# Trading Strategies From a Trading Skeptic

## Proven Techniques to Automate Your Day Trading 10X Faster For 10X the Results

Dan Murphy

Published by:

Joshua Tree Financial Inc.
2751 W Coast Hwy
Suite 205
Newport Beach, CA 92663
Phone: 866-567-4257

ISBN-10: 0989483304

ISBN-13: 978-0-9894833-0-8

Every person who has mastered a profession is a skeptic concerning it.

-   George Bernard Shaw

To my parents, and countless giants of science, and philosophy – without whose shoulders to stand upon, I would have never seen further than my own shadow

## Table of Contents

# Introduction

That's right – a book. We've all heard the rumors about how they're going the way of the dinosaur, a doomed piece of outdated technology – but not so fast.  I believe they've still got some life in them yet.  Some of you might know me through my software, seminars and webinars, but others might be wondering, "Who the hell is this Murphy character and what does he mean by an Auto-trader lifestyle?"

Within these pages I plan on answering both of these questions – first, who I am, where I come from and, most definitely, where I'm headed.  And then, even more importantly, share with you what I've learned through years of experience, through trial and error, ups and downs, and good old-fashioned dedication and hard work, all of it tempered with a healthy dose of skepticism.

I felt it was important to get all this down on paper, something you can slip into your briefcase, access on your e-reader, Kindle or iPad, so you can dip into it whenever you get the chance, at the office, at home, even at the beach (okay, maybe not the beach).

And as you can see, and feel, it's not too thick, so don't panic. We're not talking *War and Peace, Lord of the Rings*, or even *The Bible*. And yet, in its own modest way, this book may just become your Auto-Trading bible. Your manual to millions, to financial independence and a nice big piece of that proverbial pie. I'd like nothing more.

This book isn't, obviously, a who-dun-it, a thriller, or a story with a surprise O. Henry twist at the end – in other words, there's no reason to skip through quickly and race to the finish. And peeking gets you nowhere. There's a lot of complex, important material here, so take your time with it. Make it work for you.

And I'll give you another added incentive at the outset, so maybe you'll read through the book that much more carefully. I'm going to be giving away a $25,000 prize, which I call the Quant Prize, for whoever comes up with the best trading system design (and my apologies in advance, for you readers who pick up this book after the fact. Just check my website, which is updated regularly).

**Quick tip**

Visit the website now to learn more about the Quant Prize.

Point your browser to:

**www.10xtrader.com/skepticbook**

There's more on the contest at the end the book – a contest which, if the response is even half of what I'm predicting, will be the first of many. And one more thing before we take the plunge here, a confession of sorts, for the sake of candor and clarity. My modus operandi for this book, besides spreading the word about the 10X auto-trader lifestyle, is I WANT you to take this info and use it **to design a killer trading system** and **win** that Quant Prize. I want to tap your ambition and pool your talent, so we can all progress in this crazy game. I want you to quickly digest what I've learned, through years of trial and error, and make a real contribution.

Right, let's get started – and remember, you'll have a much better chance of winning if you pay close attention and take notes. As a very wise soul once said, "Time and tide wait for no one." I wonder if he was a fellow surfer?

But be warned, contest aside: within these pages you *will* learn a great deal, and if tenacious, most likely make a lot of money, while allowing you to free up more time – time to live and not work. But I offer no magic formula, and there is no Holy Grail. I did, however, stumble across a group that can predict the future. I kid you not.

They live in Italy, up in the mountains, outside the town of L'Aquila, about seventy-five miles outside of Rome. Back in April of 2009, they picked up and moved to safety three days before a terrible earthquake struck, destroying their homes. How did they sense such a portent? It seems they were able to pick up on minute changes in the ionosphere – and they were so sure of the impending danger, they left right in the middle of mating season. And they're nothing but a bunch of toads…seriously, common toads. And I say, more power to them.

I mention these actual toads – and applaud the scientists who monitored them – for a reason. Sometimes there are similar signs in the markets – minute, rippling changes which signal something greater. Rumblings within the data. You saw it in 1929 and again in 2008. And while I'm not an alarmist, per se, I see some of these signs now. But the last thing a well-prepared auto-trader should do is retreat.

During the depths of despair of the 2008 bear market I actually did remarkably well. If, like the toads, you know what to look for, you can ride out the next wave on top. It's what I plan on doing. No, I'm not foolish enough to predict the future – none of us can, with absolute certainty, in this business of trading. But it pays to be well prepared. So let's get started, and meet your competition.

# Chapter 1

*We have met the enemy and he is us.*

*- Walt Kelly, Pogo*

Within that secretive world of hedge funds and proprietary traders, there's no group more guarded, elusive, or profitable than what you'll discover here. They like the aura of mystery that surrounds them – and believe me, they want to keep it that way.

You might have heard about these traders referred to as the modern day equivalent of Wild West gunslingers, guys who bravely and boldly set out in search of fame and fortune.

Or perhaps you've seen their very sizeable footprint in the stock exchanges. Yet unlike the elusive Bigfoot or the legendary Loch Ness Monster, we have proof that this group of traders does indeed exist – and that they account for 30 to 60.8% of total volume traded on the New York Stock Exchange. That's one sizeable chunk of change, however you add it up.

The methods these traders employ – methods which make them and their clients many billions of dollars in profits – are closely guarded secrets. Secrets that an insider familiar with their inner workings and strategies would never consider sharing – until now, that is.

Some might consider me a whistleblower, a turncoat, or even a traitor. Frankly, I don't care. First, it's just plain impossible, since there is no solemn oath taken, no signature in blood, no secret ritualistic cabal. I'm not breaking any laws, either, written or otherwise.

Besides, they're not really a group in the traditional sense of the term. And they sure as hell don't share their info with each other – it's every man for himself. Yet when they go outside, it's almost always to another hedge fund. And boy, do they have clout with the banks – perks and special treatment – we're talking lots of *quid pro quo* – that smaller traders will never have.

What we're talking about here is information and knowledge – and knowledge, as we all know, is power. And why should that power be limited to a few fat cats? Why should the ways and means to become a millionaire trader be kept hidden? I sure as hell don't see why. And that's what I plan to do here. Educate you. Enlighten you. And most importantly, empower you. I'm going to blow the roof clear off this industry and reveal, for the first time, the strategies these traders employ to siphon billions out of other traders' pockets and into theirs.

But that's only a small part of the picture. So before I do that, let me tell you about an enemy that is far more dangerous to your financial health than the Chairman of the "Bored," Ben Bernanke, and the rest of the gang at the Federal Reserve.

No, it's not the High Frequency Traders. It's not the Hedge Fund managers or greedy investment bankers and Wall Street CEOs, or even those annoying, insipid talking heads spouting away on TV.

It's YOU. That's right. Take a moment and let it sink in. You are your own worst enemy.

How many times have you listened to a self-proclaimed, self-important guru tell you which stocks to buy, when the glaring, infuriating reality is that, on average, these so-called "professional" stock pickers have a NEGATIVE return. In another time and another place, these guys would be dragged from their beds by an angry, broke mob and burned at the stake. My advice – turn off the tube.

I mean, how many times have you turned on CNBC and listened to an alleged expert announce that everything is just peachy keen with the economy, only to see the stock market collapse? It happened throughout much of the 1990s, right up to the nose dive of '98 and the subsequent dot.com bust. Even worse, of course, it happened in 2007 and 2008. Five years later and we're still slogging through the remains of one nasty recession.

So how many of these analysts, these self-important, great and powerful wizards of Oz were telling you to get out of the market in 2007? The truth: maybe one in five hundred. These guys reminded me of the Pied Piper of Hamelin, the one whose music entranced all the rats and led them over a cliff. If only, in the case of these "talking heads," they went over the edge with the rest of us who got burned.

The sad reality is that most market timers severely under-perform the S&P 500 index. Honestly, you'd be better off putting your money in an ETF like SPY and calling it a day.

It's easy to blame these people. At best, they are misguided. At worst, they're liars and crooks who are out to make a fast buck, even at your expense.

But it's time to man up and move on. Every industry has its fair share of crooks, liars, cheats and delusional gurus. Wall Street, Washington DC – are they really that much different? I have my doubts.

In your day-to-day lives, you are acutely aware of this fact.

Let's say you were in a grocery store parking lot and some guy in a van offered to sell you a Honus Wagner T206 baseball card, which just so happens to be the most valuable card in existence, for a paltry $500. (One just sold in April of

2013 for $2.1 million.) My guess is that you'd tell him to go take a flying leap and peddle his BS somewhere else, and fast.

Yet you're willing to suspend disbelief when it comes to trading the markets. Your sharply-honed skepticism, all that combined book education and street smarts, goes right out the door. You start believing, wondering, hoping that there might be something to these angles and wave counts touted by dead gurus…

…or that maybe sunspots, planetary alignments or good old gravity are somehow influencing the buying and selling behavior of tens of thousands of traders.

So why are you tempted to believe them, despite their pathetic track records? It's not because you're a bad person – far from it. And it's not because you're naïve.

The reason can be found deep within you, to that spot where you hold the burning desire to be privy to the sure thing, to the trader's Holy Grail, the answer to all your dreams and enormous riches. You want to believe these people, put your finger on that magic pulse, because you're passionate about the benefits successful trading can create for you and your family – benefits that can change your life, and theirs, forever.

Take a moment and think about how often you have mulled all this over, while putting in those long hours and aspiring to:

- More free time to spend doing the things you sure aren't able to do with a regular 8 to 5 job.

- Or more money, the kind of cash that will allow you to upgrade from a coach to a first-class lifestyle: the cars, the boats...the dream house(s) you pictured yourself living in when you were younger. Or those lavish vacations in exotic locations: safaris in Africa, or unlimited shopping on the Champs Elysees.

- Above all, about being your own boss and setting your own hours. If you want to go play 18 holes of golf, go and grab those clubs.

Being passionate about wanting and leading a better life is no crime. You know that. But it's not a God given right, either. Still, it's a huge advantage these days, as fewer and fewer people seem passionate about anything outside of the realm of reality TV and five minute YouTube clips. There has never been a better time to harness that passion and live the dream.

At the same time, you know as well as I do that passion alone isn't going to cut it. You need hard, irrefutable facts and a bracing dose of cold truth if you're going to get from Point A, where you are now, to Point B, where you want to be, as a successful trader.

Okay, I'm going to go out on a limb here and assume that you're a human being and not a robot. And as a human being, comprised of flesh and blood, of heart and soul, you've been born with some amazing abilities. You've given up most of your basic instincts, those of our distant, unshaven and rather ripe smelling ancestors, but in return, your mind has the elasticity to mold itself to nearly any environment imaginable. We humans are the ultimate adaptors.

However, nearly all of us still have an instinct, buried deep within us, which is a fatal flaw when it comes to trading.

As the ultimate survivors, our instinct is to never ever let an opportunity go by. If our ancestors saw a piece of low hanging fruit dangling from a tree, they'd snatch it in a second, thinking they were the luckiest creature on earth. In much the same way, most traders will take the quick profits and be satisfied.

Those same ancestors of ours would also go to great lengths to get that ripe piece of fruit, even if a poisonous snake was hanging on the same branch as that apple. They'd figure out how to grab it, come Hell or high water, instead of searching for food elsewhere – and a few of them, you can be sure, got bitten for their troubles.

Our ancestors' basic instinct was to go after what was right in front of them… sometimes foolishly – and sometimes fatally – underestimating the risk involved.

As a trader, we often underestimate the risk of going after what we perceive to be that low hanging fruit.

We take quick profits and let our losers run.

But hold on! In trading, you want to do exactly the opposite! You want to let your winners run and cut your losses short.

Yet our instincts betray us, time and time and time again.

Like I said before, your worst enemy in trading is YOU.

If it's any consolation, you're not alone. It's a fact that 95% of short-term traders lose money to the other 5%, the ones who are able to get out of their own way.

Earl Nightingale (1921-1989), dubbed the "Dean of Personal Development" and one of the greatest motivational speakers of all time, was absolutely right when he said that if you want to ride the fast track to success, observe what the majority do in an industry and then go and do the opposite.

And that's exactly what the most successful traders in the world have done and continue to do. They've liberated themselves from the bonds of our survival instinct and taken the difficult path, the road less traveled.

By taking themselves out of the picture as much as possible, by laying low and staying silent, these traders have been able to amass a quiet fortune. Billions – yes, billions – of dollars, all in just a few short years. We know them as program traders or algorithmic traders.

In layman's terms, they use computers to trade the markets automatically. These computers, as you know, don't suffer from human shortcomings. No, they aren't smarter than people, but they are faster – much, *much* faster – and they don't make emotional or irrational decisions.

If you code a strategy into a computer, it will follow those rules without question. That computer will also tell you, in no uncertain terms, whether your ideas are worthwhile or whether you should pack it up and go back to the drawing board.

Computers do not suffer from any bias whatsoever. They are anathema to emotion. Many theories about the markets – most theories, in fact – suffer from the natural, innate biases humans possess. We hear about ideas in technical analysis that are completely subjective. For instance:

What exactly is a "double top"? Or for that matter, what exactly are the rules used to define a "top"? What is a "head-and-shoulders pattern," a "triangle pattern," or a "wedge"?

Patterns, in trading, are purely subjective. Where one person might see a wedge, another might see a triangle. Human beings are pattern recognition machines. We see patterns in everything…even in randomness.

Don't believe me?  Look up into the clouds overhead, on a clear sunny day. What do you see?  One of you might see a face, another maybe a crouching animal or a docile sheep. Yet those exact same cumulus, to another passerby, will be a dead ringer for a car, a piece of fruit, maybe even Marilyn Monroe. The bottom line: No two people think – or see things – exactly alike.

Creating significance out of randomness is a phenomenon known as pareidolia. It's the basis for the Rorschach inkblot test, which tries to gain insight into a person's mental state by asking them what they see, when all they're really looking at are, obviously, nothing but a bunch of ink blots. Our brains try desperately to make sense of the world, and far too often this desire, this ingrained need, fools us into seeing patterns where there are none. And that's why…

**…technical analysis, for us traders, is dead!**

In fact, it was dead on arrival. It never had a prayer or a hope in hell.

When I said this to a group of traders in a packed conference room, the uproar was deafening, the anger palpable. How dare I speak such heresy? How could tens of thousands of traders be so wrong for so many years?

To which I responded, quite calmly: "It's simple: **every scientific theory is eventually disproved and replaced by another.**"

Remember, it used to be common knowledge to think that the world was flat, the earth the center of the universe and the sun actually revolved around us, until the likes of Kepler, Copernicus, and Galileo were able to prove otherwise.

There was a time, not all that long ago, when it was accepted knowledge that the Earth was only five thousand years old, as stated in the Bible. Today, it's widely considered to be roughly four and a half *billion* years old, give or take 1%.

Then, of course, the greatest scientific minds in the world believed that Newton's theories on gravity were written in stone, until a twenty-five year old German physicist named Einstein came along, waving his theory of relativity.

I'm no Einstein, but then again, it doesn't take an Einstein to know that technical analysis isn't even a scientific theory. Since no two people see patterns in exactly the same way, you can't have a repeatable experiment.

My favorite trader of all time, Ed Thorp, realized this back in the 1960's, when he started one of the first hedge funds, Princeton/Newport Partners. It's really worth taking a moment and paying due homage to a great mind.

In fact, Ed, who was also a distinguished mathematician and an expert gambler, whose book, *Beat the Market* (1967) helped launch the derivatives revolution that transformed securities markets, took the viewpoint that markets were mostly random; that what we see as patterns are like the clouds I described earlier. That viewpoint allowed him to extract wealth from the markets at a blistering pace, with an annual rate of return of 20 percent over nearly thirty years. Not bad, folks.

The guy's amazing – and is still around, by the way, a chipper octogenarian living in one of the greatest places on earth, Newport Beach, California. Ed, who Forbes referred to as a "card shark," was able to figure out, in a single day, that Bernie Madoff's operations were pure fraud – and this was back in 1991! You can read about it in Scott Peterson's *The Quants: How a New Breed of Math Whizzes Conquered Wall Street and Nearly Destroyed It* (2010).

How I wish I'd found Ed years earlier in my trading career. You see, fresh out of the classroom, I was listening to the majority, the accepted, already outdated wisdom spout on and on about wave counts and trend line breaks. I studied *Technical Analysis of Stock Trends* by Edwards and Magee and dozens of other books, hundreds upon hundreds of pages that simply copied their work. And that book was written in 1948!

Here, by the way, is what Ed had to say about *Technical Analysis*: "[It] was very helpful in the negative. I didn't believe it. The book convinced me that technical analysis was a road not to go down. In that sense, it saved me a lot of time."

Ouch! You guys don't know how fortunate you are. I'm here to save you time. I had to bear professors who drove rusty old Honda Accords while talking outdated, irrelevant drivel about how to make money. To be fair, I don't hold anything against these professors – their hearts were certainly in the right place and they were just playing it by the established rulebook. And in a very real way, these professors were simply teaching what so many financial advisors out there right now, their hands tied by the ropes of regulation, are actually applying – these ridiculous models. So yeah, count your blessings.

I had to get out of there. So rather than continue calling E*TRADE for quotes between classes, I dropped out senior year and became a full-time trader.

## Horse Racing Millions

Needless to say, I wasn't making money as a young trader, green as a leprechaun on St. Paddy's Day. You know that guy at the poker table who doesn't know he's the sucker – that was me. We're talking 1997, the height of the tech boom, and everyone, it seemed, was getting rich – fast! Who wouldn't want in, right? So in I went, with a splash...

...And blew out two accounts, very quickly. I made one of the worst moves imaginable – I traded on my credit cards, losing a couple of grand in the blink of an eye.

But then I had a proper epiphany, a certifiable and timely "aha!" moment. It dawned on me how my grandmother's uncle Clarence would handicap horseraces, something I watched him do, riveted, back when I was a real little kid. The man, I later learned, was able to make millions playing the ponies, where most everyone else lost their shirts and sometimes their sanity.

I was so young when I knew him. He lived in Sacramento, and he was the first person to teach me about spending money. Once, a group of us kids went with him to Dillon Beach, California, and he had my mom give me $1. This was in 1979 – I was all of four years old back then – so a buck went a lot further. I bought candy (of course) and he helped me count, and I knew I should get 25 cents back, but I got a bit less, and immediately thought I'd made a mistake. And then he taught me about taxes, which I thought were dumb (still not a big fan, by the way).

There was a pomegranate tree in front of Uncle Clarence's house. I loved eating those seeds, but it was a pain to get those little buggers out. He taught me to use a knife and spoon to get the treats out. Watching him simply pound those little suckers out stayed with me, in ways I wasn't aware till much later.

Generally, instead of simply following what everyone else did to tackle a problem, I'd think about it for a bit and see if there was a better way. When I started applying that philosophy to the markets, I started to see glimmers of success. It was a bumpy road, but I persisted, keeping the example of Uncle Clarence close to heart (and mind).

I used to visit Uncle Clarence a lot back when I was still in elementary school, and sit quietly and watch him go through his facts and figures, for hours on end: who each jockey was and his record, and how each horse performed on various track conditions…these were real world numbers, tangible variables and hard facts, not chart patterns or wave counts.

Uncle Clarence did everything by hand, with a pencil and yellow note pad. No calculators and certainly no computer back in those days.

Back then, as a naïve, wide-eyed kid, I thought it was some kind of game or hobby. I had no idea he was able to become so wealthy from gambling. He had a modest house and car. He was retired, and led a simple life. Looking back on it, I think he just liked playing the game because he was so good at it, that it brought him some sort of internal satisfaction. The money was clearly secondary, an afterthought, little more than proof that he really was a master of what he did, because he was willing to take a risk.

After rediscovering my roots, courtesy of my epiphany about Uncle Clarence, I decided to use a computer model for all my trades. I didn't have the money for custom software back then, so I made my own. I wrote a program in PERL that could back-test some strategies. I made a computer model that could time the S&P 500 fairly well back in the late 1990's. But I still suffered from the emotional problems that come from trading, and proceeded to blow out an even larger account.

Eventually, I got more sophisticated with better software and I would at least tread water by breaking even. Then I learned that my back-testing was faulty because I wasn't using out-of-sample data. That's data the computer never gets to look at. Then you compare the two and make sure they are similar. I wanted to see answers on whether to buy or sell, in black and white, not fifty shades of grey.

It took a while, I can tell you. At first, I made a lot of mistakes. For instance, I would "curve-fit" or "over-fit" the data, which means if you're willing to poke and prod the data in enough ways, it will eventually tell you what you want.

This isn't much more than mathematical wishful thinking, like Cinderella's stepsisters trying in vain to slip their big ugly feet into the glass slipper – and the results of my real world trading looked nothing like it did in the testing phase.

Sure, I was frustrated. But steadily, slow and sure, tenacious and determined, I learned more and more about the ins and outs of computer modeling, until, after six months, I had not one, but several systems that worked. To this day, in fact, I'm still using their basic framework to pull money out of the markets, just like Uncle Clarence did at the racetrack.

For the next few years everything was fine and dandy, and, flush with hard-earned funds, I decided to take some real time off. What I thought might be a month or two turned into a fantastic year and a half, where I traveled to places I'd always wanted to – all across the States, Europe, the Caribbean – and met a lot of amazing people, including a few unforgettable women. I put my feet up whenever I felt like it, brought my golf handicap way down, and generally had a great time. No regrets at all.

But then, one day, I came across an article on trading. Specifically, on automated *day* trading – the topic I've been working up to here.

## What Not to Do: Manual Day Trading

As I mentioned, I'd tried my hand at day trading over the years, and even came up with what I thought was a decent system for day trading the E-mini S&P 500. My system went like this:

Look for the market to be trending up for the day and about to make new highs, then anticipate a breakout and buy right before the prices made new highs. The edge was that a bunch of orders would pour into the market as stops were hit, since everyone and their mother would place their stops one or two ticks above the high of the day. In a few seconds, all those stops would automatically turn into market orders, driving the E-mini even higher…at which point I cashed out for two to four ticks of profit.

This was back in 2002, when I had no idea how to automate or even test the strategy. Truth be told, it wasn't much of a system, since it was still susceptible to all the problems, which make us poor humans such innately horrible traders, by following our instincts. So even though it was profitable, I abandoned my trading method. It was 83% winners, but the loss size was slightly more than the average win size.

Looking back on this strategy, it's likely that I would have eventually blown up if the market moved against me suddenly. I probably would have not sold if the S&P 500 went down three or four points all at once. It could have just kept going down. Don't ever forget that markets can suddenly turn at any time. You won't even know what hit you.

But there's more to it than that, with me. I have a confession to make, and one that might sound crazy given what I do for a living…

...I hate looking at charts all day. That's right, downright hate it. My eyes were so strained from staring at that damn computer monitor all day long; they were red and dry, My back hurt from being hunched over my desk like some Quasimodo; there was a nagging stiffness in my neck that was hard to get rid of. I got burned out very quickly doing this. Where would I rather be? That's easy enough: playing a round of golf or hanging out at the beach when the surf's up, catching rays and the occasional killer wave.

A decade ago, auto-trading was still sketchy. Data interruptions were the norm, and losing your connection could wipe you out if you were trading on the heavy margins, the way I used to. At one time I was trading off a 56k modem. And remember that scratching sound when you dialed into AOL? Then it was cable and DSL. Sometimes there'd be outages when everyone was using bandwidth at the same time. The software also had lots of small problems. And those weird, inexplicable errors or worse, the blue screen of death. Windows used to shut down for no reason. The horror.

If I had just left it at that, as a burned out, frustrated auto-trader glued to his desk, I wouldn't be where I am today, as an expert in automated trading. Folks, I would have folded up my tent a long time ago. But I wasn't about to give up – and neither should you. Harness that inner tenacity. Never fold up or give in. Never stop researching, testing, trying – and don't be afraid to fail – or mark my words, someone else will eat your lunch. And chances are you'll spend the rest of your life regretting your decision to toss in the towel. I know I would have.

Everything I've talked about until now – about human instinct, about how each and every scientific discovery is destined to be replaced with another, that everything is in flux and, sorry, there are no magic beans – has been for a reason. I've been clearing away the debris and preparing a solid foundation from which you can build your own trading business. Notice I said trading "business." This will come up later on. But let's take a moment here to pause and review.

By now, you should be familiar with these key points:

1) The majority of traders are not just wrong, but completely misguided as to the inner workings of the markets. Much like people used to think that the earth was flat, most traders believe prices move on fundamental information. They are delusional because they haven't adequately tested their ideas – and they haven't tested their ideas because their rules are simply too loose…too subjective…too haphazard…and let's face it, downright hopeless.

2) Our brains try to make sense of all the stimuli thrown at it, even to the point of finding patterns in randomness…such as looking at clouds…or subjective chart patterns such as those outlined in Elliott Wave Theory and other forms of technical analysis. No two traders will see the same patterns, therefore testing whether they work or not is not possible. As Ed Thorp discovered in the 1960's, it's a waste of our precious time.

3) Our natural instincts for survival make us horrible traders. We tend to take profits quick, and let our losers run. But true success means doing exactly the opposite.

4) In order to get out of our own way, let computers do most of the tasks when it comes to trading.

Congratulations. You are now primed and ready – and hopefully pumped up – for the advanced portion of this book. This, ladies and gentlemen, is where fortunes will be made and lives changed for the better. (And who knows, it might just help you win that $25,000 Quant Prize I'm giving away, for the best trading system design). Okay, let's get this sucker into high gear and dig deep into the realm of automated day trading.

# Chapter 2

*A successful man is one who can lay a firm foundation*

*with the bricks others have thrown at him.*

*- David Brinkley*

## A Day in the Life of an Automated Trader

Imagine waking up after a good night's sleep. You get up, feeling refreshed. You brush your teeth, deal with some basic biological needs, get the blood pumping with some brisk exercise, and then eat a full, healthy breakfast, just like your mother taught you.

At this point, most people are scrambling to check their emails and the latest news, or else rushing to get out the door to fight traffic on their way to the office for at least eight hours. But not you. Instead, you proceed to read for the next 30 minutes as you take time out for yourself. No work, no Internet, no TV. Just relaxing with a book, starting your day stress-free.

Once it gets close to 9:30AM New York time, when those markets open, you pick up your laptop computer and fire up the Remote Desktop program to log into your dedicated trading server thousands of miles away.

In about five seconds, you see two buttons lit up green like a Christmas tree. As always, your dedicated server is wired into Tradestation's servers. You're fully locked and loaded. Over the next minute or two, you look at the futures markets to get a snapshot of what the opening will look like…and, as usual, there's nothing dramatic going on.

So you log off your remote session, check emails, surf the news, the sports page, and take care of any pressing issues. This will be the last time you'll need to check any emails until later in the day. I mean it – stay away from those emails when you can, since they're the biggest time waster I know.

Right, now it's nearly 1PM EST, New York time. You're near the 8th tee and you park your golf cart in the shade, so you can see your iPhone screen a bit better. (You don't need your laptop on the golf course when you've got a smart phone with the latest version of the Jump app to link up to your auto-trading server.)

Looks like your systems made you a couple trades today. You're up $2342. Sweet! You'd be up nearly $3400, but one of the trades was stopped out after a half hour for a quick loss. But you shrug it off; that loss doesn't bother you. You know that it's all part of the game.

Tradestation is still connected to the data and trade servers. You're still in an E-mini S&P 500 trade from earlier this morning, which is showing a profit. But you resist your old instincts, knowing better than to take a quick profit. You close the app and let the systems do what they were vigorously tested to do: Make you money with little or no human intervention.

Right, back to the green to finish 18 holes, and then down to the beach, where the swell is going to be a foot overhead, according to the surf report. Better swing by the house to pick up your wetsuit and surfboard.

Fast forward to 4:07PM EST, with the markets in New York poised to close. Your iPhone alarm went off while you were driving home –damn traffic – and you're walking in the door a little late. The surf was amazing and you let the time get away from a bit too much. You flip on the laptop and log in. All lights are green, but you see a little alert box in Tradestation. "Crap!" Looks like the server disconnected and then reconnected itself, the first time this has happened in months.

Hey, no problem. Crap happens, right? So rather than panic, you fire up the TradeManager and see that the position from earlier this morning wasn't sold. With a click of the mouse, you're out, and all strategies match your real trading account. Your closed profits for the day are way up – $5207 – even with a rare hiccup.

Your trading day is done, your money's been made, and you were able to enjoy 18 holes of golf, followed by enough time left over for catching a few waves.

Does this sound like a lifestyle you could get used to? Replace the golf with some tennis or basketball, maybe a 3D matinee at the Cineplex. Take in a museum, escape with a book, or indulge in a long lunch with that special someone. What's important isn't what you do with all this extra free time, it's about having it. So you have to ask yourself: Does it sound too good to be true?

Sure it does, but it is attainable. I should know. The story is 100% true. I should know, since I lived it – and I have been for many years now, day in and day out. I trade every single day, in a real account with real money. I run dozens of strategies simultaneously on a server in New York. Most days, there are absolutely no data disconnects. In fact, most days are pretty darn boring, but to be fair and realistic, I wanted to tell you about a day where there was a trading glitch. They do happen, after all.

This lifestyle of mine wasn't invented overnight. No genie granted me this wish. It took me several years to figure out the magic formula for auto-trading my account. Want to know what it is? I thought so.

The magic formula is that there is no magic formula. It's all about hard work and testing, so you don't end up fooling yourself. A new system trader wants desperately to find that eureka "quit my job tomorrow" trading method – and he'll fool himself at all costs. But deep down, in his heart of hearts, he knows, like me, that he should be testing more…but come on, that would kill the fantasy, and we know how tempting that is.

But with me, check your fantasies at the door. Not only must you come up with strategies that work here, in the real world of trading, but you must also know the best equipment and software setups, because without them, you can kiss the hands off approach good bye.

What I'm going to do next is give you a huge head start into automated trading with the proper setup. Come on. Let's dive right in.

## Setting Up a Dedicated Server

Setting up your automated platform is one of the most important things to do, so let's start there. Consider this your foundation. It needs to be put together with great care, to bear the weight of what's to follow, as you construct your auto-trading castle.

First, you need a dedicated server. There is absolutely no substitution here. Period.

Take it from me, as I learned this fact the hard way, after losing over $10,000 in a single day...a day where I should have actually been up $2000. Ouch, right? You've been warned. Don't let it happen to you.

Back in the day, I thought I was a master of the universe, 100% certain in the knowledge that I had everything covered. I ran my trading software from my laptop, allowing me to be mobile. That Dell laptop of mine went with me everywhere, even on several vacations, part of fine-tuning the lifestyle we all want to live. Not only could I have a main Internet connection from my home or hotel, but I also had a backup data service that worked all the over U. S. I used that baby on a killer vacation right on beautiful Wiki Beach. And if those connections didn't work, I figured I'd just haul ass to the nearest Starbucks or Internet Café.

For a long time, this was working fairly well…until one day something went wrong. I point the blame squarely on the fact that I'd grown too over-confident on my setup.

I was in Austin, Texas, visiting a buddy. This was a guy's only trip, which for me equals playing a ton of golf. (In another life, I plan on winning that green jacket in Augusta, GA.) If memory serves, I wasn't quite the Tiger that day, shanking a drive well into the woods and almost taking out a poor deer. I blamed it on the large amount of adult beverages we consumed that day. Remember, it was vacation time.

At about midday, feeling no pain, I whipped out my now antique smart phone and tried to log into my laptop. But I couldn't. Frustration set in. Was there service? Sure enough, full bars. Web pages were opening fine. A feeling of sobering dread rushed over me, and I considered sprinting back to collect my laptop.

But I didn't want to be a party crasher, so I waited it out, tried to let it go. It wasn't my best round of golf, believe me.

By the time we got back, I was in full panic mode. Sweat on my brow, heart pounding. Back in those days, I was trading on big margin. My Tradestation account was only in the low six figures, but I was trading 40 to 50 E-mini S&P 500 contracts at a time! Talk about crazy.

Long story short, my laptop had crashed, completely. There was some kind of bug with the software that controlled the data card. After rebooting and firing up Tradestation this felt like an eternity, while I circled around my laptop, cursing the damn thing), I discovered I was down over $10,000 because a short trade hadn't closed out. Immediately, I flattened all positions.

A long time ago I learned that if there's ever a glitch, just get out immediately. Doing anything else – holding on in desperation - is just hoping the market will go in your favor. And hope is an emotion, it's thinking with the heart, and doesn't belong anywhere near your trading, which requires a cool head at all times, particularly when things are looking dark.

When I got back home, it was back to the drawing board. My once brilliant plan was suddenly shattered into a million pieces. The experience also taught me a lesson about using insane amounts of margin. We traders need to expect the unexpected. And that experience in Austin back in 2007 proved invaluable. Better still it was priceless, because it proved to be the difference between me profiting during the Flash Crash of 2010 or being wiped out (I'll deal with this in more detail later on).

After extensive research, I decided to setup a dedicated Windows server on Go Daddy. As of the summer of 2013, you can get a pretty supped-up server with plenty of RAM and bandwidth for $170 per month. And that's money very well spent, especially when you consider the potential costs – that

is, LOSSES – you risk without it.

The process is pretty simple: All you have to do is use

Remote Desktop to log into the server and it's just like it's

right there next to you. All modern Windows computers have

Remote Desktop installed. You can even download it for free,

if you're a Mac user like I am.

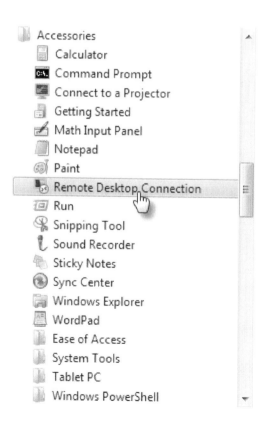

Okay, here's what's so cool about this setup:

- Your computer is now in a server farm with constant power.

- A thief might make off with your home computer, but good luck getting past their security.

- Mega-fast T3 connection to the Internet. Losing a connection is extremely rare, and trades go through that much faster.

- No need to carry around a laptop. Simply login with your iPhone in virtually every country on the planet.

- If the server crashes (which I've never seen happen), you can reset it remotely through a web browser.

And FYI, not only does a dedicated server give you peace of mind, but the cost of that one losing trade, thanks to some infernal bug, would have paid for fifty-eight months of fees. That's five years of sleeping soundly at night, folks…and no telling how many disasters averted.

## Staying Connected Worldwide

Back in 2007, I bought my first iPhone, and it quickly became both a blessing and a curse. The curse is that I was now connected to the Internet and all it entails – email, text messages, Facebook, friends and family – around the clock, 24/7.

We all know how it is…if someone texts, you'd better answer in five minutes or less. No excuses. I read a study that stated how multi-tasking on your phone and the constant interruptions can make your IQ fall lower than if you were smoking pot. I believe it. On average, each interruption will set you back fifteen minutes before you "reboot" into work mode.

Luckily, you can train your friends and family not to expect a response. As an automated trader, you absolutely must do this now, so you can live a peaceful and interruption-free lifestyle. When was that? That's right – Now!

Obviously, there are a whole lot of positive things to say about having a smart phone or I sure wouldn't own one. If you're away from your home or office computer (which, as you know, I highly recommend doing whenever possible), you've got your trusty phone with you to log into your dedicated server.

For the iPhone, I use an app called Jump, which works better than all the others I've tested, and will only set you back $14.99. I can log in from just about anywhere, provided I can get a signal through AT&T or Wi-Fi. If you're deep in the jungles of remotest Borneo, you're probably screwed, but given the way things are going in most countries these days, technology will only get better and better in that regard. It's one of the few things I'm willing to bank on.

What amazes me is how quickly – and completely –
this kind of technology has changed my life, personally and
professionally. Trust me, it will change yours as well, so let's
continue.

## #1 Software to Use

Now that you have a foundation that promotes the auto-
trading lifestyle, let's talk about which software to use.

There are several choices, naturally, and I'm sure there
will be many more to come. Heck, there are already several
I'm going to leave off this list, but that's because I only talk
about what I've tested.

Searching for the right infrastructure took me several long years, and as I noted before, I had to learn a lot of tough lessons in the process, so this should save all of you that most valuable of all commodities, time.

When it comes to dealing with technology, there are, fundamentally, two different classifications of people:

There's the Windows Guy and the Mac Guy. The Windows guy wants control over every last function. He wants to customize and configure to his heart's content. Then there's the Mac guy, who doesn't want to fool with anything. He just wants to turn the damn contraption on and let it work its magic, on its own.

As for me, I'm a total technology nut, if you didn't already guess, but I fall under the Mac Guy persona. My days are done tinkering and screwing around with every last detail. I'll hire other people to customize if it's absolutely vital. After all, if you're going to take on the auto-trading lifestyle, you're well aware that customizing is a time vampire.

Time isn't just money. Time is your life. And speaking of your life, it's time to talk about something I've spent the last several years of mine developing, sometimes by accident, more often by design, but always with passion. It's become my *raison d'etre*, my reason to be. Read on to see how and why.

## 10x Trader Lifestyle™

I coined a name for life as an automated trader. I call it the **10x Trader Lifestyle™**. It's about you working 10 times smarter so you can make 10 times more money, at 10 times the speed, all while having 10 times more free time and fun. Why save up to retire when, if you follow my plan, you can effectively retire right now? Technology has brought this gift to our front door. All we have to do is open it.

With that said, here's what I'm using right now: Tradestation. And no, I'm not affiliated with them. I believe strongly in staying impartial.

They've been around the longest and have the largest following. They're time tested and true. Launched back in 1991, at one time they were a public company, but were bought out twenty years later by Monex, one of Japan's largest financial provider firms, and have been private ever since. They win best platform awards left and right, given by Barron's and a bunch of others, so I'm not the only person giving them rave reviews.

As far as automation goes, Tradestation has a well-thought out and highly developed system for dealing with data disconnects and position mismatches. You'll get these on occasion. Take it in stride. It's part of the 10x Trader Lifestyle™.

Tradestation is loaded to the gills with technology, but don't be intimidated, their stuff is super easy to use.

Tradestation is an all-in-one solution. They provide the data feed for quotes, and you use them for order execution. If you do enough trading – and I hope you guys eventually will – they wave the platform fees. Fees change all the time (usually for the better, since it's a competitive world), so check out their website at Tradestation.com.

Last time I checked, you can't open an account at Tradestation from every country, so I'll discuss that later on.

There are three other software vendors I've used, such as Multicharts, NinjaTrader, and MetaTrader. Multicharts is basically a Tradestation clone, using the same computer code, *Easy Language*. Multicharts would be my second choice. They aren't a broker or quote provider, so you would have to seek out multiple sources for that.

The other broker I can recommend – again because I've used them – is Interactive Brokers. They're a large firm, based out of Greenwich Ct, with revenues at around the $1 billion mark, and with clients from around the world. You can use Multicharts to easily place automated orders with them.

NinjaTrader, headquartered in Denver, CO, allows you to configure to your hearts delight, but I must admit, it's not for me. It's made by techies for techies, so proceed with caution. One of the biggest problems in using a different quote vendor than your broker is this: the symbols can be different. This means going in and manually mapping each ticker symbol to your broker's symbol. And that, as you now know, does not fit into the 10x Trader Lifestyle™, unless of course you hire someone to take care of it for you, leaving that time for living.

Trust me, once you've got a thoroughly tested system, it's really EASY it is to automate your trades. Have a look:

You simply turn on a few switches. First you right click on your chart with your strategy on it. Click on format strategies. Then check the "Generate strategy orders for display" box. Then check the "Automate execution using "yourfuturesaccount #." Read the warning and click "I agree" if you understand the risks. Next, you select "account with confirmation" to "Off".

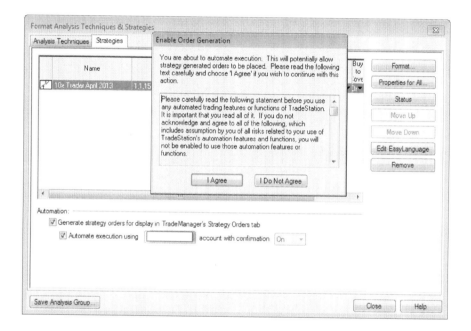

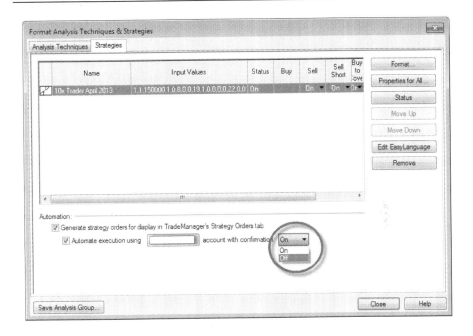

If you are using more than one system per futures
contract, then you click on Properties for All on the right hand
side and select the Automation tab. Check the box the says
"Allow multiple automated strategies on multiple charts
using the same futures/forex symbol in the same account."
I use many different strategies to trade several markets, so I
always check this box.

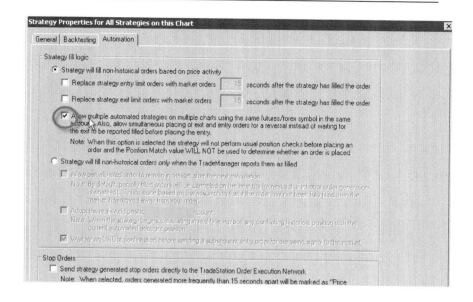

Sometimes your data stream will disconnect or you will be disconnected from the Tradestation network. This can cause your systems to miss trades. Tradestation has two types of nag screens to let you know when something has gone wrong. Most of the time, these disconnects will last 1-2 seconds.

Here's a list of recent disconnects. There are a few that lasted several minutes, so being out of sync with the market is a real possibility and is why I recommend checking your trading computer three times a day, **especially at the beginning and end of your trading day**.

Having a trade server located on a server farm greatly reduces data disconnects. This is a snap shot from my home PC, not my trade server ...and I pay for my cable company's "highest" level of service! Not all these network errors are caused because of Tradestation.

| Info | Price | ▽ | Date & Time |
|---|---|---|---|
| Established Data Connection | 0 | | 4/13/2013 11:47:32 PM |
| Disconnected from TradeStation | 0 | | 4/13/2013 11:47:28 PM |
| Established Data Connection | 0 | | 4/13/2013 9:17:20 PM |
| Disconnected from TradeStation | 0 | | 4/13/2013 9:17:16 PM |
| Established Trading Connection | 0 | | 4/13/2013 6:17:41 AM |
| Established Data Connection | 0 | | 4/13/2013 6:17:40 AM |
| Disconnected from TradeStation | 0 | | 4/13/2013 6:06:01 AM |
| Disconnected from Order Execution Ne | 0 | | 4/13/2013 6:06:01 AM |
| Disconnected from Order Execution Ne | 0 | | 4/11/2013 4:16:04 PM |
| Disconnected from TradeStation | 0 | | 4/11/2013 4:16:03 PM |
| Established Trading Connection | 0 | | 4/11/2013 1:50:05 AM |
| Disconnected from Order Execution Ne | 0 | | 4/11/2013 1:50:04 AM |
| Disconnected from Order Execution Ne | 0 | | 4/9/2013 12:58:37 AM |
| Disconnected from TradeStation | 0 | | 4/9/2013 12:58:37 AM |
| Disconnected from TradeStation | 0 | | 4/8/2013 6:10:19 PM |
| Disconnected from Order Execution Ne | 0 | | 4/8/2013 6:10:18 PM |
| Disconnected from TradeStation | 0 | | 4/7/2013 5:34:02 PM |
| Disconnected from Order Execution Ne | 0 | | 4/7/2013 5:34:02 PM |
| Established Trading Connection | 0 | | 4/6/2013 6:19:32 AM |
| Established Data Connection | 0 | | 4/6/2013 6:19:29 AM |
| Disconnected from TradeStation | 0 | | 4/6/2013 6:07:59 AM |
| Disconnected from Order Execution Ne | 0 | | 4/6/2013 6:07:59 AM |
| Established Data Connection | 0 | | 4/5/2013 11:52:46 PM |
| Disconnected from TradeStation | 0 | | 4/5/2013 11:52:36 PM |
| Established Data Connection | 0 | | 3/30/2013 11:49:32 PM |
| Disconnected from TradeStation | 0 | | 3/30/2013 11:49:28 PM |
| Established Trading Connection | 0 | | 3/30/2013 6:18:26 AM |
| Established Data Connection | 0 | | 3/30/2013 6:18:25 AM |
| Disconnected from TradeStation | 0 | | 3/30/2013 6:06:28 AM |

So yes, trading has become comparatively easy, but always be prepared for glitches. It's part of my trade smart philosophy. And now comes one of my favorite questions:

## What to Trade?

For auto-trading, there are many routes you can go: Futures, Forex, stocks, options, etc. But when you boil it down, there is only one route that makes the most sense, and that is futures trading.

The problem with stock trading is that the government has gotten way too involved. We've got regulations through the roof, intrusive, debilitating, and sometimes downright insane. There are few things governments can actually solve, in Washington, London, Tokyo, you name it. Politicians everywhere are like most people: they attack a problem head on. If that worked, there wouldn't be a problem in the first place. **The most obvious solution is rarely a solution at all.**

In an effort to protect you – an educated, hard-working adult – from yourself, regulators have decided to reduce the amount of margin you can use. Short selling is often frowned upon and taken away. Besides, it's hard to borrow some stocks to sell short anyway.

Oh, and did I mention that you need at least $25,000 to day trade?

That's all fine by me. If you trade stocks, you should know that they are mostly correlated to each other anyway. You'd be better off, in my book, by just trading the index.

Options, however, have been making a definite comeback. Day trading options is doable, but the bid/ask spread is often high, while liquidity is often low. To be honest, options tend to attract amateur traders with little money…much like slot machines attract people dependent on social security. Sorry, but that's the sad truth.

At its core, the 10x Trader Lifestyle™ is about saving you time and aggravation. Therefore, you want to trade during a fixed interval. It's okay to sacrifice some potential profits in order to have fewer headaches. Don't forget, it's about quality of life. Futures and Forex can trade nearly 24 hours a day, so it's necessary to limit the hours you are going to take a peek at the markets. Otherwise, you'll become a prisoner, obsessed, stressed, overworked, and missing out. And that runs contrary to the 10x lifestyle.

Despite the high dollar amount traded in the Forex market, no currency pair has the liquidity of a futures contract to match the E-mini S&P 500. Most of the time in the Forex market, there's $70,000,000 in orders at the immediate bid and ask…sometimes more. I can't budge that market.

Forex is like the Wild West without a true exchange to trade on. Like the options market, it tends to attract small amounts of money from traders with, you guessed it, small amounts of money. And brokers, believe it or not, often trade against their clients. Not for me – not at all.

So let's go "back to the futures." The futures markets offer tremendous liquidity, have tight spreads, more than enough margin, trade on an exchange, and therefore lend themselves ideally to the 10x Trader Lifestyle™.

Futures, remember, trade similar to stocks. The main difference is that they're based on different assets, such as gold, or oil, or the S&P 500 index. There are other differences, too, but this isn't the place to list them.

These facts are the reason that trading futures is the appropriate choice for the 10x Trader Lifestyle.™ Equally important, in my mind, is that the futures market also filters out those that are looking to get rich quick. I wouldn't touch a futures trade with less than $20,000. Your broker will want you to have $50,000 in liquid assets just to start an account. For this reason, I mostly find myself helping those who are already successful.

The markets are mostly a trap for everyone else – and like all traps, you should avoid them like the plague, or risk entering at your own peril. You've been warned.

## Using Multiple Systems

One of the biggest cons perpetrated on would-be-successful-traders is that there is, supposedly, one secret method out there that you will allow you to find, trade, profit from and then retire rich, beyond your wildest dreams. Traders call it the Holy Grail. Listen up, people: **It does not exist. In case you missed that, let me repeat, in the strongest possible terms, in bold, capital letters: IT DOES NOT EXIST.** I hope that's clear enough for you – and believe me, more than a few have almost died trying to find that sucker.

Hey, don't take it personally. Even professional traders have been duped by this fallacy. I remember a group of grain traders that minted money for decades from pairs trading. They would short one grain and buy another when their spread was far apart. There's a fancy word in statistics –

"covariance" – that explains that behavior, which is the measure of the degree to which returns on two risky assets move in tandem. Eventually, this "system" stopped working for these guys, and guess what, they either left or went broke.

The lesson here: markets evolve and change because the people trading them evolve, quit, or die off. Therefore, you should always adapt your trading as well. If you don't, you'll meet the same fate.

And just like evolution, the quicker you can adapt to change, the better off you'll be. Even better, would be to expect and anticipate change. That will get you to the top of the food chain.

One way to do this is to trade multiple systems on many different types of assets, all at the same time. For example, you can trade gold and oil with automated trading systems that look for breakouts or you can trade the S&P 500 with systems that look for both mean reversion and breakouts.

By diversifying your trading account with several different assets and trading styles, you will automatically be doing two things: First, enjoying a more consistent and steady uptrend in your portfolio, and second, also enjoying a higher reward to risk ratio.

Amateur traders think in absolute terms: for instance, "How much did I make last year?" Pros, on the other hand, want to know how much you risked in making those gains. If, say, you made 40% on your account and had a drawdown of 80% to get there, that's totally unacceptable by professional standards.

Here's a quick question for you: What's better, Portfolio A, which makes 20% and has a 10% drawdown, or Portfolio B, which makes 40% and has a 30% drawdown? Most amateurs will answer the latter, B, because the absolute percentage is higher. But they'd be wrong. Portfolio A has a reward-to-risk ratio of 2.0 while Portfolio B has a reward/risk ratio of 1.33.

Trading futures offers tremendous leverage, which is why absolute returns mean nothing without factoring in risk. I could make 1000% a year with a 90% drawdown, but I'd probably get an ulcer, for one thing…and one day I'd be wiped out. And that's precisely the kind of thinking that does NOT fit into the 10x Trader Lifestyle™.

That kind of thinking reminds me of a trader I watched once in a trading contest. He won a lot of live contests because he would keep doubling his position every time the market went against his position. It's known as the Martingale strategy, and you see it all the time at the Blackjack tables in Vegas. And it's the reason why they set table limits.

Eventually, you blow up in spectacular fashion, like the Hindenburg, because the market keeps moving against your position; but to the untrained eye, it looks like you're a trading deity, with divine knowledge. It's a classic example of a Taleb Distribution. Lots and lots of winners, and then poof, the market pulls the rug out from under you.

Nassim Taleb, an author and hedge fund manager, probably explained it best in his seminal book, *The Black Swan* (2007), with this turkey analogy: Imagine you're a turkey, he wrote, and you've eaten well and lived in safety every day of your life. For one thousand days and counting, everything in your experience tells you that tomorrow will be no different. You are fed, you are warm, you are happy. But then Thanksgiving arrives…and *wham!* the butcher barges in and cuts off your head. Lesson: The unthinkable can and will happen.

To keep your portfolio from being decapitated by the market, you should avoid strategies that seem to defy statistics. This includes option-writing strategies that win 90% of the time, only to crash and burn every few years.

If you're trading a position on margin, you should ALWAYS be using stops to limit your risk.

You should use many types of systems.

If you went fishing, for instance, wouldn't you be more likely to catch a fish if you had ten different lines in the water?

You should be trading several liquid markets, such as the S&P 500, gold, oil, and bonds.

You don't just go to one spot to fish. You go to several. Increase those odds.

# Chapter 3

*It is far better to grasp the universe as it really is than to*

*persist in delusion, however satisfying and reassuring.*

*- Carl Sagan*

.

**System Ideas: What's Working Now**

At this point, you should have a pretty clear idea regarding the do's and don'ts of trading.

Now it's time to get more specific and talk about trading methods that I use, day in, day out, to pull money from the markets. I'm going to focus specifically on the S&P 500 since it's the most liquid and volatile single market in the world, and simply the best place for you to start.

I'm not going to cover the basics here. I suggest you go to the CME's website for all that (www.cmegroup.com). With that in mind, let's begin.

## Mean Reversion

The S&P 500 is mostly a mean reversion market. In other words, if price goes too far down, it tends to snap back up to its average price and vice versa. This mean or average can be the historical average of the price or the return, or even another relevant average such as the growth of the economy or the average return of an industry. There are many ways to take advantage of this.

The first way I'll demonstrate is a trap, so take heed, but it clearly illustrates my point about the S&P 500 "mean reverting" the majority of the time.

Pull up a 45 minute chart of the S&P 500 E-mini. Now calculate the average distance between the high and open of every bar. There are ten 45-minute sessions during the regular session, so let's use that for the average. Call this value "the high Average."

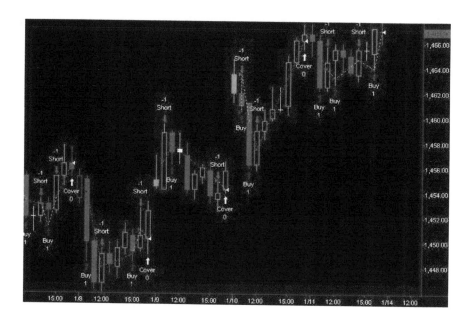

Next, take the average between the opening and low of each bar. Call this the "low Average."

That's basically all you need for this trading method. Again, I have to tell you that I'm proving my point. You see, this system doesn't work, for reasons I'll share a little later on.

But for now, let's pretend the system does work. You'd simply skip the first 45 minutes of trading. At the close of that 45-minute bar, you'd place an order to buy at the close of the 45-minute bar minus the low Average. You'd also place an order to sell short at the close of the 45-minute bar plus high Average.

Once one of these prices is hit, you'll ping pong back and forth between long and short all day…and finally, just before the close of the session at 4:15PM New York time, you go flat.

Here are the results of that strategy over the past 10 years:

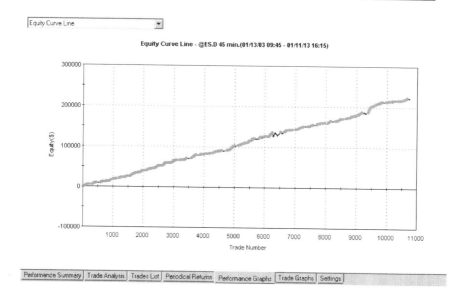

I know, this looks like a damn good strategy on paper, and it does prove my point that the S&P 500 mostly cycles up and down all day long. This graph also proves my point that you don't need to hit a few grand slams to make a fortune in trading. You just need to get thousands of base hits.

The reason this system doesn't work is because it assumes you would be filled when the price hits your limit order. You won't every time, because it's very tough to buy on the bid and sell on the ask.

I also didn't factor in commission and slippage. Slippage, which I discuss in more detail later, is due to you buying the ask and selling the bid. For example, the close of a bar might say 1500, but your fill was likely 1499.75 on the E-mini. Some call this "trading friction." Typically, you can count on paying about $30 "roundtrip" in most futures markets. Roundtrip means entering and exiting a position. So if I buy one E-mini contract at 1500 and sell at 1505, that's a roundtrip. And you will definitely get slippage with this system because you won't be getting filled when you think you should. Better get used to it.

Here are the results of the system with a more realistic model of how it would perform in the real world:

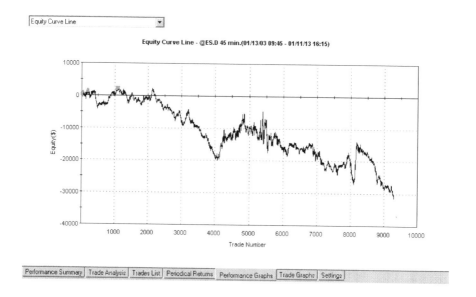

Yuck! Watch out everyone. Don't fall for this testing trap or your portfolio -- and your 10x Trader Lifestyle™ -- will go up in a puff of smoke. Gone with the wind.

Now let's look at a system that uses "mean reversion" and works.

It's pretty clear what a big fan of testing I am. Call me a groupie, even. I cannot overemphasize this. I can't get enough of testing. And the main reason I don't trust what others say is because 99% of them never test a thing. Just because someone believes in something strongly doesn't mean they're right. Santa Claus, the Tooth Fairy...oh yeah, and the trader's Holy Grail.

For years, I listened to traders spout off about Fibonacci numbers. For those of you who aren't aware of what these are, here's a brief explanation:

The roots go back to Italy before the Renaissance, where one Leonardo Pisano Fibonacci, a traveler like Marco Polo, picked up an ancient Hindi system of nine symbols and, eventually, developed these and other mathematical concepts in a book called *Libre Abaci*, published over eight hundred years ago, in 1202. There is some real valuable stuff here, believe me. His "golden ratio" can be seen throughout the natural world, in terms of honeybee populations, sea snails, and even with its ability solve a sum about the propagation of rabbits. It's amazing stuff, really.

It's only when you try to apply this to trading that my red flag rises. So guess what: the Fibonacci studies won't provide you with that magic solution or lead you to Nirvana.

How do I know?  Simple: unlike a lot of folks out there, I tested it – and tested it.  So when it comes to trading, do NOT let them serve as the basis for your decisions. There is simply no place for such psychological comfort in the trading world I'm letting you in on.

But I'll confess that for a while I thought they might be on to something, since, as I've already demonstrated, the S&P 500 likes to "mean revert," and buying "pullbacks" – a decline in price – could potentially be profitable.  Where do we want to buy when a market starts declining?

Well, traders buy pullbacks at 23.6%, 38.2%, 50%, 61.8% and 78.6%.

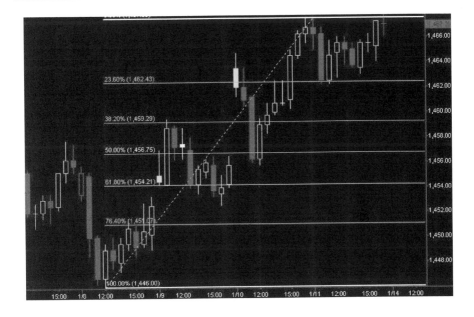

And this brings us back to the main problem with Fibonacci ratios. Even if price doesn't reverse exactly at one of them, a trader will still fool himself into believing it was the Fibonacci number at work. Why? Because deep down this trader felt that a magic solution was at hand – but if you remember anything here, remember that such solutions don't exist. Never had, never will. These ratios are created by us, by mere mortals, in our vain attempt to dispel uncertainty.

Say I kicked a football and it landed at the fifty yard line. Would that mean a Fibonacci number was at play? It's the same thing with trading.

So what I did was let the computer tell me which levels are best to buy after a big up day. I didn't get a Fibonacci ratio. In fact it was between 23.6% and 38.2%.

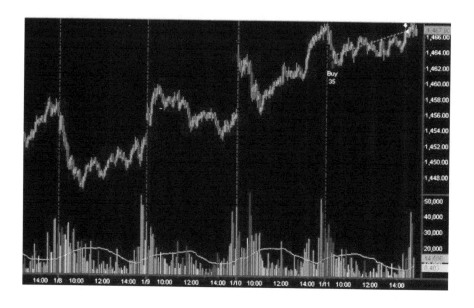

The system would then buy at this ratio using a limit order and then set a target and stop loss so the potential risk and reward were exactly the same. Here are the results:

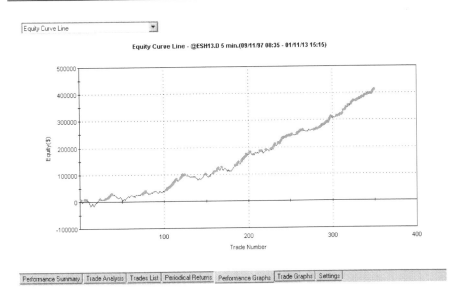

As far as I'm concerned, the only edge traders are utilizing when buying Fibonacci retracements is that stock indexes like to mean revert most of the time. I've also tested this on daily data and high frequency tick charts. The tick charts did show an exact Fibonacci level that worked (the 50%), so I haven't completely dismissed it from my trading arsenal.

## Volatility Breakout

I've really been cheerleading the fact how most of the time the S&P 500 is just gyrating back and forth like Elvis Presley's pelvis back when the King was a young buck. But that's not always true.

Actually, the S&P 500 will sometimes behave in totally the opposite manner. Sometimes, it will trend all day long. No, it's not schizophrenic, it's just… unpredictable. Those days of upside down volatility are the ones when the Martingale traders get their heads handed to them with a big grin – from me! Ear to ear. I've made a lot of money exploiting this fact.

If you're going to test ideas about the markets, first come up with actual ideas to test. And in order to do that, there's no substitution for keen, unblinking observation. And if you're not a keen observer, then it pays to be a keen listener.

I didn't come up with the volatility breakout method. The VB system I designed was based on 20% observation and 80% listening to other traders' ideas. Let's dig a bit deeper here.

Remember to think of volatility as a measure of range. One commonly used formula for volatility is average true range, or ATR. ATR takes the difference between the high and low of a bar and finds the averages based on how many price bars you're looking at.

For example, the "true range" here refers to the cases when there are price gaps. Instead of taking the high of the bar minus the low, you take the close of the *previous* bar minus the low. And don't worry: all of the software packages mentioned have this function built in, so no, you won't have to reinvent the wheel.

And when we're talking volatility breakout, we mean that the ATR is expanding, with the sizes of the price bars getting larger and larger.

I used to spend a great deal of time at the old Newport Beach library, which they've since replaced. It's where I played tennis and did the lion's share of my research. They had a basketball court there, too, and I'd shoot for hours on end, running ideas for tests through my head, as if I were in a trance, with no idea how many shots I'd taken.

One day, on the stacks, I came across an old dog-eared book that was highlighted and marked up with notes. Normally, I get ticked off when someone writes in a library book, but whoever wrote in this book was a freaking genius. What a find!

The observations by the author were fantastic (for the record, it was Toby Crabel's *Day Trading With Short Term Price Patterns and Opening Range Breakout*, published way back in 1990 and now out of print, though I've seen copies on Amazon for anywhere between $400 and $1000). But the notes clearly pointed to a working trading model that I just had to test immediately.

I bolted from the library as fast as I could, speeding like a maniac, top down, foot to the floor, a man with a mission, the entire way home. How could I explain this to a traffic cop? There was no wife in labor next to me, but I couldn't contain my excitement. Luckily, I made it home without incident and bolted straight to the computer, with one of those mega-size 7-11 coffees, put on the headphones, cranked up a bit of Techno music (appropriate, right?) and preceded to program non-stop through the night, dusk till dawn. Yeah, I was tenacious.

By the next day, I had a working trading model. The secrets spelled out by Crabel and the mysterious note-taker provided the breakthrough I was looking for. Crabel was so meticulous in discussing trading the opening range breakout (ORB). Even back then he was looking at 5-minute bars. What stood out to me wasn't really that markets would keep trending a certain direction after a big move up or down. It was that I should only **take the signals early in the day**. That made a huge difference in my testing. With today's modern computers, I've taken Tony's work to another level, which we'll delve into later on, with genetic algorithms and switches.

I dubbed the system I developed *Thermite*. Why? Because once you ignite thermite, it will cut right through solid steel, like a hot knife through butter. Once this pattern starts, price will blow through everyone's stops for the rest of the trading session.

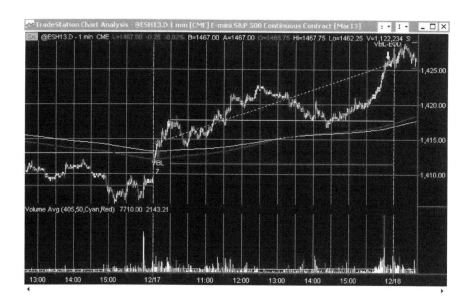

I now saw how price would often continue in the direction of a breakout. What most would consider an "overbought" market, Toby showed, through extensive testing, that

the index would often continue to defy logic and head higher
and higher. The notes I read added that extra edge I was
looking for. Here are the most recent results:

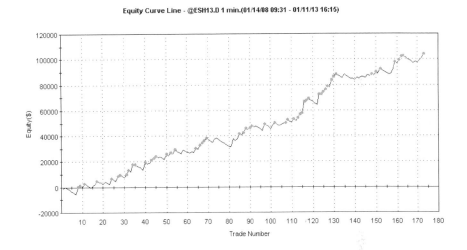

# Chapter 4

*Two roads diverged in a wood and I – I took the one less traveled by, and that has made all the difference.*
*- Robert Frost*

**TICK Data and Trading**

So far, I've been covering edges that you could find through careful observation of price and time charts. You can find many edges in the markets this way. But there was something that a master hedge fund trader, William Eckhardt, once said that has always haunted me:

He basically said that trading edges come from non-linear relationships that statistical estimators can't pick up on. My take-away was that he was referring to functions such as highest, lowest or median, but his comment sparked something. He might just as well have been referring to non-linear time data.

Back in the 1980s Eckhardt was Richard Dennis' trading partner. They were also known as the Turtle Traders because of an experiment they did to see if people were either natural born traders or if they could be taught to follow exact rules. These guys only traded systems, back when you had to use punch cards to test ideas. They went on to spawn an entire generation of trend followers. They'd buy the highest high in twenty days in a commodity like oil, then sell the lowest low in ten days. It worked really well during the insane inflation of the 70's and early 80's. Eventually others caught on and it doesn't work so easily today.

In our modern age of high-powered computing, which shows no signs of slowing down or flattening out, why should we look only at a price chart with a fixed time interval? I could look at each and every trade if I want to. Every trade – or "tick" – has a time and a price stamp on it. I can group several hundred trades together to make a price chart where time is now non-linear.

Look at an intraday chart and you'll notice that most of the volume occurs near the open and close of the day, while during the middle of the day, trading dries up. But if you use "tick charts," the price action looks much more consistent. In fact, pattern recognition algorithms are much more accurate when you get rid of time as a factor in trading.

To illustrate my point, the charts on the next page are from the "Twitter Crash" of 2013. A fake news release of explosions at the White House and an Injured President Obama sent the markets tumbling within seconds. The top chart shows a quick spike down on one-minute data, and a

492 tick chart on the bottom. Notice how the tick bars give much more detail. Using one-minute bars is like using a scalpel on a patient, whereas the tick charts are like using a laser.

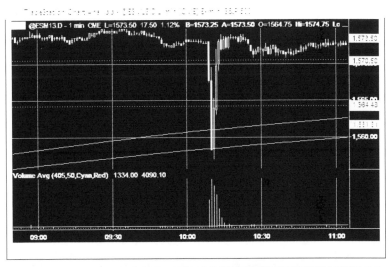

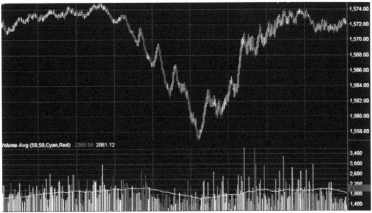

## Finding Serendipity

In 2008, I added tick charts to my trading arsenal. It was one of the most volatile periods of trading I've ever seen, before or since, in my career and in the history of the markets. I remember it like it was 9/11/2001. Yup, it was that bad. The selling was relentless: selling begot selling. Margin calls. A vicious cycle. Idiots were leveraged 30:1 and a lot of managers knew it.

This is why I pound the table on lowering the amount of risk you are taking. That way you survive to trade another day. Back in 2008, the music had stopped playing and everyone was scrambling for a seat.

At that time, I just so happened to have recently started a trading blog to chronicle my million-dollar challenge, which was to turn $10,000 into $1 million. Here are the results:

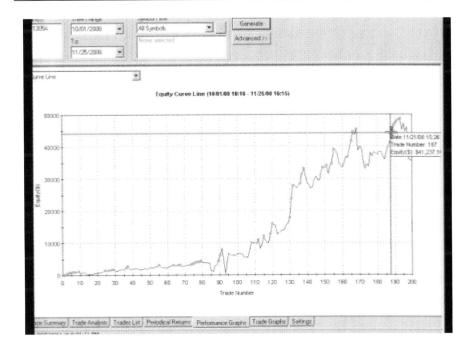

Over a period of 38 trading days, the account was up $41,237, or near a 100% gain. By the way, this is a real account with real dollars, not hypothetical testing. While most were in a state of panic and proclaiming the end of capitalism, I was making money. It felt pretty damn good.

The system was actually an accidental discovery, as many important ones are. I wanted to see if and how I could take advantage of the pristine patterns that emerge from using tick charts. I also wanted to combine this with the facts already mentioned about the S&P 500 mean-reverting most of the day.

I ended up inadvertently transposing two numbers and...voila! I had this beautiful trading model that could pluck money out of the markets like a pickpocket on a crowded subway train after the bars close.

## A Bit More on Tick Charts (It's Worth It)....

By the time I'd created my automated pattern matching system (APM), in 2010, there wasn't enough data to give any significance. Here, in a nutshell, is what APM did: It looked at modestly high frequency data in the E-mini S&P 500 (around, say, 450 ticks), then toss out all the data except where tops and bottoms were in price. After this, the algorithm would compare the current pattern to all historical data – and we're talking real time here, aka, a fraction of a second.

Why so quickly? Simple: because I'd stripped away 98.6% of the data. Remember, most of it is noise anyway. If the real-time back-test had numbers I could live with (such as a profit factor > 1.7 and a return/drawdown ratio > 9), it would place a trade. Bingo. Done.

I would only get around 100 samples, which in real trading flat out did not work. I shut it off just a few weeks before the flash crash. Now if I had more data at that time, I would have wanted many, many more trades.

Here's a simple "rule of thumb" check for statistical significance, one that I borrowed from electronic engineering:

$$confidence = \frac{signal}{noise} \times \sqrt{sampleSize}$$

You can substitute signal/noise with your system's profit factor. Profit factor is very similar to a signal to noise ratio. (Winning trades * Average win size) / (losing trades * average loss size). Using profit factor is much more important than just looking at winning trades.

Amateur traders want a high win percentage because it makes them feel good about being right. I could care less. The number of winners, as you can see from the previous formula, is just one quarter of what you should be looking at. Most of my systems win between 50-70% of the time…with most being closer to 50%. And how do they make money? Easy: the average winning trade in much larger than the average losing trade, often by a factor of 2-1.

Getting back to significance… Let's say your profit factor is 1.8. Now if I had 300 trades, the confidence level would equal:

$$1.8 \times \sqrt{300} = 1.8 \times 17.32 = 31.18$$

Now take a look at what my APM system was getting for its confidence level with only 100 samples on average. No calculator needed, you can do it in your head:

$$1.7 \times \sqrt{100} = 17$$

Oh boy. That's not even close to what I want to see. Instead of six months of data, I need at least eighteen months. And if you're like me, you'd actually want ALL the data…or at least going back to October 5, 2009 when the CME changed their aggregation rules. Anything before that time is not the same data you're getting today. Right now – the summer of 2013 – I can potentially get 700+ trades, which, frankly, is excellent. The square root of 700 is 26.46…which is almost to the magic number 30 all by itself.

## Advanced Strategy: Timed Limit Orders

I also had a really cool trick up my sleeve to maximize profits. Pay very close attention here, because this simple trick has made me thousands and it only takes a few seconds to implement.

What I did was use a special Tradestation Automation function. When my strategy recognized a profitable pattern, it placed a buy limit order one tick below the close of the current bar. If that limit order didn't get filled in five seconds, it automatically turned into a market order. Most of the time, my limit order was filled.

The minimum move (or tick) on the S&P 500 is 0.25. That tick is $12.50 per contract. That extra tick in profits might not seem like much, but each one can add up to a house payment.

Now before you go running to your computer to test out tick charts, I'm going to tell you about a few of the hurdles you must overcome first.

## Tradestation Wish List

Tradestation is really quite cool for charting and automation – unlike anything I've used before – but there are some features it lacks. Hey, nothing's perfect. And fear not, I'll tell you how to overcome them without too much effort.

Back in 2008, I was lucky to start using tick charts when I did. Tradestation only allows you to download six months' worth of tick data. That was fine in 2008-2009, when the markets were going haywire. There were lots and lots of trades. After the markets stabilized, there was much less data in those six months. For instance, in October 2008, the 20-day average peaked at around 2.8 million contracts. A year later, average 20-day volume was 2.0 million.

In today's trading, there is a solution to all of this, but you're not going to like it. You need to buy data from a 3rd party. More than that, it's going to run you about $500 up front and $125 a year for maintenance *for each symbol*. Keep in mind, however, that this isn't a necessity to get started. It's something I highly, I mean *highly* recommend for advanced traders.

 **Bonus tip**

Visit the website now to point you to my recommended data vendors.

Point your browser to:

**www.10xtrader.com/skepticdata**

You've heard this from me before, but I'll say it again: the more difficult it is to accomplish something, the more profit potential this something has.

It strikes me as funny, as in odd, when people balk at the relatively small costs of their trading education when you compare them to the cost of an average college education.

The average price tag per year, for a public college here in California, is $22,261. The price skyrockets to $44,289 per year for a private college. And that's just tuition and room and board. Then you've got books, transportation, incidentals – a few grand more, for sure.

That, to me, is downright ridiculous. You can get started in trading for much less of an investment, and it can pay off so much more quickly if you take all the lessons I've been teaching you to heart and mind. The 10x Trader Lifestyle™ can last a lifetime. It's not something you need to retire from some day. It's there for you, always, providing a great way to make large sums of money.

Next on my Tradestation wish list is a real-time position sizing formula. I'm a bit surprised that neither they nor their competitors include one. When markets are going crazy, you should be trading with less money. That's just commonsense.

All of my trading models have built-in money management that I custom coded myself.

All I do is tell the computer that I don't want to risk more than 1% of the account in a losing trade, and it looks at my real-time account equity and adapts automatically. This is trading smart, letting the tools do the work.

**Bonus tip**

Visit the website now to download my trading system template.

Point your browser to the link below:

**www.10xtrader.com/skeptictemplate**

I even take this a step further.

I told you how important it is to trade many systems and several markets. Let's say, for example, that you have thirty systems and they all decide to fire off at once. It's extremely unlikely you would be stopped out of all thirty trades, but it pays to assume the worst. Amateur traders think aggressively – about how much they can win. Seasoned professionals are defensive – they think about how much they can lose.

Sometimes, during a crisis, unrelated markets start trading together in lock step. We saw that earlier on, and it's something professional traders know all too well.

And this is why having some sort of position limiter is so important when trading multiple systems. The limiter keeps you from having too many positions open at once. Maybe you want to only be exposed to a 10% loss if everything moved against you. Amateur traders stop adding positions when they run out of margin. Professionals stop adding when they've hit their predetermined level of "portfolio heat," which is the sum of all the risk you have assumed by placing trades. Imagine if each open position's stop triggered at the exact same time. This is your portfolio heat, as coined by world-renowned trader Ed Seykota of *Market Wizards* fame.

If you risked 1% in ten positions, your total portfolio heat is 10%. If suddenly and unexpectedly the markets become correlated and go against you, you could lose 10% (or even more – much more – if the market becomes jammed with orders, like it did during the 2010 Flash Crash).

You could go a step further and reduce exposure by asset type. Let's say you trade three trading systems each on the S&P 500, NASDAQ 100, Russell 2000, Dow Industrials, Midcap 400, and DAX, and don't want more than 5% exposure in this index as a group. Theoretically, you could be exposed to 18% portfolio heat if all these systems fired off at once. The position limiter takes care of this instantly, efficiently, and more importantly automatically, by acting as a gatekeeper after the 5% exposure limit has been reached.

It's impossible to lead a 10x Trader Lifestyle™ when you're constantly worrying about your exposure to the markets. Automating your exposure to risk is absolutely worth the expense. A good programmer can do this for around $1000 for a setup I am sure you'd be more than happy with.

Yes, you can still auto-trade without this extra piece of software, but as you become increasingly more profitable and your account grows well into six figures and beyond, the position limiter is critical. Like the turkey, you can get away without it for a long time, but one day, the market will come for your head.

# Chapter 5

*The difficulty lies not so much in developing new ideas as*

*in escaping from old ones.*

*- John Maynard Keynes*

### The Future of Automated Trading

When it comes to technology, there is one thing you can bet the ranch on – it'll keep changing very rapidly. Most people look at technology's break-neck speed and shake their heads, stating that they have no idea what's coming next.

Yet we do know the growth rate of computers. According to Moore's Law, microchips become twice as fast every two years. This exponential growth has made it possible for the transistor count to go from 2300 in 1971 to 2.6 billion in the 10-core Xeon chip from Intel. This stuff boggles the mind.

At current speeds, computers can now process HD video in real-time or even play against human opponents on Jeopardy – and win.

The recent bump in computing power has created new fields of science, such as artificial intelligence, or AI.

In ice hockey, the greatest scorer of all-time, Wayne Gretzky, credited his success not from skating to the puck, but from skating to where the puck will be.

In developing trading systems, I've always used a computer to do the testing. Back in the day, I used a brute force method for testing different variables, which was slow and time consuming, but still much better than doing it by hand.

Then someone came up with the bright idea of using algorithms basted on evolution to speed up the testing process, sometimes by a factor of 1,000,000 or more. The difference was like night and day.

If we're going to "skate to the puck," as Gretzky put it, we must be on the lookout for new technologies that will take advantage of not only faster computers, but also quantum leaps in ideas.

## Survival of the Fittest: Speeding up Back-testing Through Genetic Algorithms and Genetic Switches

As you've guessed by now, having made it this far, I'm something of a Darwinian trader. It doesn't mean that I'm ruthless, unless by that you mean ruthlessly realistic. One must adapt or perish – it's that simple. And yes, like it or not, only the fittest survive. And I do prefer analogies from science and the natural world to help understand what we're up to here, and not just because they're entertaining but because they actually teach us something.

So imagine my delight when I first learned that algorithms were developed that were dubbed "genetic," followed by the fact that thanks to technology, courtesy of the computer, we can actually use these algorithms for trading. These algorithms are based on the concept of, yes, natural selection. It's as if Darwin himself was invited to ring the opening bell at the New York Stock Exchange. It doesn't get much better than this.

In a nutshell – or a banana peel – we're now able to become better traders by harnessing the power of nature. But as we move ahead, never forget my warning that there are no Holy Grails – and that includes genetic algorithms. With this in mind, let's take these GAs a step further.

In the early days of computers, when they were as big as a linebacker, it was difficult and extremely time consuming to create systems with multiple inputs. As a result, most systems were very simple, like calculating two moving averages. When the fast moving average crosses *above* the slow moving average, it could signal a buy; and when the fast crosses below the slow, a sell. And that was that.

Later on, you could use back-testing software to find the number of periods to use for each moving average. A typical test might step the parameters for the fast moving average from 5 to 100. The slow moving average could be in the 50 to 300 range.

If each parameter is stepped by one, the computer must do $(100 - 5 + 1) * (300 - 50 + 1) = 24,096$ calculations.

That might sound like a lot, but a modern computer can do these calculations in under an hour with a reasonable amount of data.

But what happens when, in your search for the optimal trading system, you have an idea with several inputs that must be stepped? Let's say you want to find a specific time of day to buy the E-mini S&P 500. That would be one input. Next, you'd want to put in a protective stop based on average true range (ATR). Your stop would be entered as a multiple of ATR, with the ATR's formulation based on a number of periods, similar to the moving average example above.

From there, you might want to find the ideal time to sell the position. And while we're at it, it's probably not a good idea to buy at just any old time, so maybe you'd want to setup the test to "buy only" if, for instance, the market has fallen by a number of ATR over a certain number of periods.

Oh boy…now you've got six parameters to deal with. Let's say you were doing this test for the nearly 24-hour session on the E-mini S&P 500, with 15 minute bars. Just look at all the tests that must be done by stepping each input:

Inputs

1) Time of day to buy (Step from 0-93 by an increment of one)

2) ATR periods (30-200 by an increment of ten)

3) Stop loss multiple of ATR (2-10 by an increment of one)

4) Time of day to sell (0-93 by an increment of one)

5) Down momentum periods (4-120 by an increment of one)

6) Minimum down momentum ATR (0-5 by an increment of 0.5)

Here's the number of tests that must be run: 94 * 171 * 9 * 94 * 117 * 12 =

19,092,440,016!

That's right, any back-testing software must run over **19 billion** tests. Now imagine doing that on ten *years* of E-mini data. If each test only takes 30 seconds on a modern computer, it would still take **18,162 years** to finishing testing! I don't know about you, but I need something just a tiny bit faster.

Thankfully for us, there is a way to speed up the process by a factor of millions: It's called genetic algorithms.

Genetic algorithms use nature's process of natural selection to breed a trading system with the best "fitness," with fitness being the measure of the performance of each test. Typically, you could use such things as Net Profit, Profit Factor, or Win Percent as a measure of fitness.

Tradestation has their own measure of fitness called the "Tradestation Index," which attempts to give a higher score to systems with more winning trades, more profit, and a smaller drawdown. And, since the name of the trading game is to maximize your gain to pain ratio, the Tradestation Index is one of their better fitness measures. I also like the fact that it gives weight to the number of trades, but don't think it's prudent to put so much focus on winning trades. Remember, a system with a poor win percentage can still give you amazing returns, provided its winners are much larger than its losers.

Let's take a look at the Genetic Algorithm back-testing application in Tradestation. Notice that you can click on the Suggest buttons and it will give you its estimate of parameters to run.

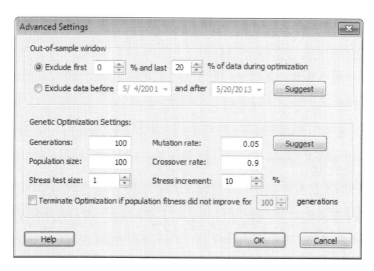

Notice that there are many different settings. Don't worry, I'm not about to write a treatise on how genetic algorithms work, since volumes have been written on the subject already. Instead, since this is all about making you better traders, I'll show you what I do to speed things up lickety-split.

Basically, there are two numbers you should be the most concerned about: The population size and the number of generations. The number of tests to be run is simply the population size multiplied by the number of generations.

Typically, I'll set the population size to 100. What this does is seed the population with random numbers from the inputs we want to step. The computer then calculates the fitness of every member of the population. Those in the population with lower fitness will be less likely to pass on their "genes" to successive generations.

Since you and I are given a finite amount of time here on Earth, I typically set the number of generations to 100 as well. That's 10,000 tests. Often, the back-testing software will estimate that it will take days to complete all the tests. In the initial testing phase, where I'm simply throwing data at the back-tester and seeing what sticks, I'll typically start the test after the market has closed, then take a quick look later that night to see if the idea has any merit.

Using this example on the E-mini NASDAQ 100, I'll let the test run for a full 24-hours before it converges on a good set of inputs. There's always a chance that there was a better set of inputs for the system, but the results were more than acceptable, as you can see from a casual glance at the equity curve. Note that I used 20% out-of-sample in this test, so I could check if my system was over-fitting the data.

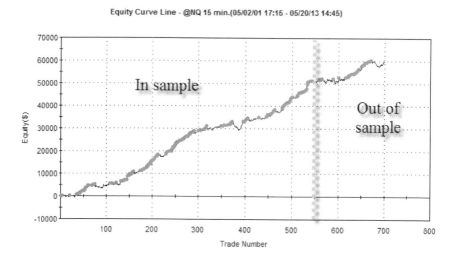

Equity Curve Line - @NQ 15 min.(05/02/01 17:15 - 05/20/13 14:45)

As you can see on the proceeding chart, the out-of-sample test of the data was very similar to the in-sample. The likelihood of this system continuing to work into the future is not 100%, but our careful testing has made the odds for continued success much greater.

Now I want to show you what an over-fit model looks like. There are two charts. One created from optimizing the trading rules of a system on in-sample data:

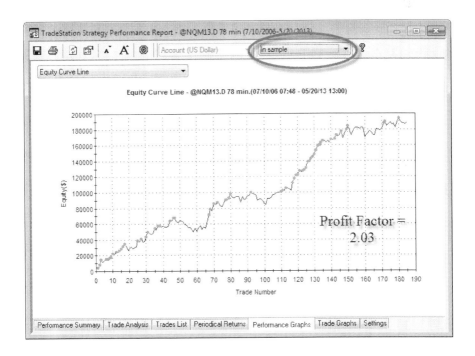

Next, I selected "Out-of-sample" to see the results of the system on data it never saw during testing.

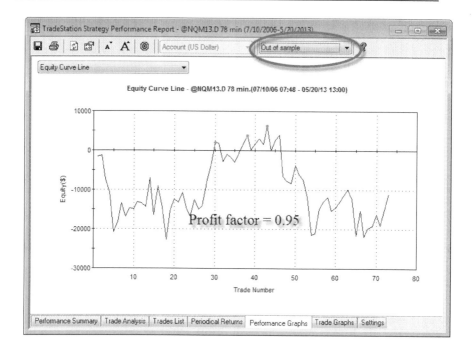

Houston, clearly we have a problem here.

With the out-of-sample results dramatically declining from 2.03 to 0.95, I believe we have to toss this into the trading system cemetery and bury it six feet deep. This isn't the first time I over-fit the data with trading rules that didn't actually provide any edge whatsoever, and it won't be the last. Use this example as yet another warning of trading system design gone bad.

Earlier, I introduced a formula for statistical significance. It consisted of a signal to noise ratio multiplied by the square root of the number of samples. When converted to suit our needs for ranking a trading system, the equation looks like this:

$$Profit\ factor\ \times\ \sqrt{NumberTrades}$$

Let's think even deeper about what we really want out of our trading. I want to make as much money as possible, with the least amount of drawdown as possible. Let's add that ratio to our equation above.

$$Profit\ factor\ \times\ \sqrt{NumberTrades}\ \times \frac{NetProfit}{MaxDrawDown}$$

But wait, I just showed you the necessity of using out-of-sample data in your testing. Let's introduce yet another ratio: the out-of-sample to in-sample ratio of profit factors. Ideally, in-sample and out-of-sample profit factors would be the same, which wouldn't help or hurt the score I'm introducing you to. However, if the out-of-sample doesn't come close to the in-sample data as I demonstrated earlier, the Trading System Score will suffer.

Here is the complete equation for the trading system score:

$$Profit\ factor \times \sqrt{NumberTrades} \times \frac{NetProfit}{MaxDrawDown} \times \frac{OutOfSamplePF}{InSamplePF}$$

Here's an example using data acquired from a day trading model on crude oil I created recently:

$$1.77 \times \sqrt{550} \times \frac{146235}{6738} \times \frac{1.80}{1.77} = 916$$

The higher number, the better. There is no easy fix to rank different trading systems, but this equation, in addition to setting certain minimums such as number of trades, will get you where you need to go.

I suppose I could stop right here, happy that I've pointed you in the right direction for back-testing. Hey, I've just outlined a working trading model that could, potentially, make you tens or even hundreds of thousands of dollars, all with only minimal effort and time. Not bad, right?

But we've got to dig deeper, to find the truly gargantuan pockets of gold in the least amount of time. You're game, I bet. So let's go back to the example I used above, where we wanted to find the best times to buy and then sell, when momentum was negative. We also added a simple stop, just in case the market moved against our position.

Now what if I wanted to test a sell target? Or a trailing stop? What if I completely reversed the rules and looked for the best time to buy with momentum rising? There could be dozens of these types of rules. We need to work smart, right? So let me ask you: is it smart to keep manually testing all these rules, or should we figure out a simple way to let the computer do all the heavy lifting? I thought so. But how?

Enter **Genetic Switching**. Here, instead of manually testing each idea, we simply write the trading code and choose whether or not to test the idea by turning a parameter on or off, like a light switch. It might look something like this:

**Switch1**: Use "trailing stop" (Step from 0 to 1)

**Switch2**: Use "sell target" (Step from 0 to 1)

**Switch3**: Use "buy stop" (Step from 0 to 1)

**Switch4**: Use "Momentum with direction" (Step from -1 to 1 by an increment of one)

**Switch5**: Use "above/below moving average" (Step from -1 to 1 by an increment of one)

**Switch6**: Use "correlation data1/data2" (Step from 0 to 1)

**Switch7**: Use "volume filter" (Step from 0 to 1)....

And so on. The list is as endless, actually, as your imagination. It's important to note, however, that the more switches you use, the longer it will take to find a solution. I certainly wouldn't want to test every idea all at once. It's so much easier to build one piece of an engine at a time, rather than all the pieces all at once. With genetic switching, I like to test several entry methods before moving on to test different exit methods.

```
⊟ // Entry condition set to true. Must be disproved
   entryValid = 1;
   entryShortValid = 1;

⊟ // Close > moving average
   If (s1 = 1) then
⊟     Begin
⊟         // Is the close > moving average?
          if  (close > average(close, var4)) then
⊟             begin donothing = 0;
              End
⊟             Else begin
              entryValid = 0;
              end;
          end;
```

Notice how, in the code example used above, the variable called "entryValid" is set to 1 right from the start. Now every time an "on" switch is encountered, the Easy Language® code checks to see if the statement is true. For example, the switch could be checking if the price is above a moving average. If true, then nothing happens. The computer simply moves on to the next switch. But if the switch was turned on and the statement was false, "entryValid" is set to zero; it doesn't matter what happens at any other switch; "entryValid" can never be equal to 1 until the next bar. No order will be placed on the current bar.

```
If (Marketposition <> 1) and

    (entryValid = 1)
    then

    Begin
```

The few lines of code above are checking to see if the system is already in a long position. If not, it then checks to see if the entry condition switches were all true. If entryValid = 1, then the system code that follows places the entry order for the next bar.

I've found that there are very good solutions to beat the markets, using very simple rules. Why not build yourself a template of these rules, and then tackle each individual market? After all, Magellan and other explorers didn't have to build a new compass each time they voyaged out to sea. And you shouldn't have to rebuild either.

 **Bonus tip**

Access my next complementary webinar where I show you how to build a working trading system from A-Z, live, including lessons on using genetic switching to cut down your design time from months to days. You get to keep the system we design in class, as well as the template I use for every day trading system I design.

Point your browser to:

**www.10xtrader.com/skeptictraining**

The key here is to tackle as many liquid markets as possible. The more markets you trade, the more often you'll be making trades and, possibly, making a fortune in the process. The added benefit of trading many markets is that when one system is misbehaving, the others take up the slack, resulting in much more consistent performance and smaller drawdowns.

# Forward march!

Now that I've laid the groundwork for both out-of-sample testing and the use of switches, let's talk even more advanced techniques.

Let's face it; as scientific, skeptical traders, we want to know if the systems we design are going to work into the future. After all, we're sticking our necks out, putting real money on the line. Are we going to profit from the fruits of our labor, or are we going to end up like the turkey with its head cut off?

Luckily, there are tools and techniques that exist to give us some degree of comfort. But I'm sorry to tell you, dear reader, no tool exists that will tell you the future. The future is unknowable despite what the psychics, palm readers, and fortune cookies claim.

There is yet another myth I must dispel at an appropriate time. I believe that appropriate time is now, so listen up. Market behavior drifts over time. Your trading rules will not work forever despite claims to the contrary. Traders grow old and die off or retire. Markets move from being in vogue to being shunned like a leper with five arms. Perhaps it's a good thing that so many hold onto this delusion. It's very likely that we stand to gain much more than the vast majority of traders if we learn to embrace this philosophy right here and now.

Markets drift over time, which means your trading system will eventually break down. It might take 12 months, or 12 years, but it will happen. From order comes chaos, and vice-versa. Next time you go to the beach, build yourself a sandcastle. Without the constant upkeep of adding water and patting down the walls of your castle, it will crumble back into its natural state as grains of sand. Eventually the elements will reduce your sandcastle to ruin.

The first idea that might come to mind on how to fight back against the inevitable is to re-optimize your system. But how often would you re-optimize? How much data would you use? Those are questions that can be answered using walk-forward optimization.

WFO, as it's known, can often help a "broken" system become profitable once again. Its powerful algorithms can be like a dying man taking a sip from the Fountain of Youth. By feeding your WFO software the stepped inputs of your trading model, it can adapt to ever-changing market conditions. For an example, I've included a screenshot of the inputs I tested for my Thermite day trading model on the S&P 500:

| Strategy | Input | Start | Stop | Increment |
|----------|-------|-------|------|-----------|
| _Thermite | stopAtr | 3 | 10 | 1 |
| _Thermite | shortStopAtr | 3 | 10 | 1 |
| _Thermite | startTradingTime | 1 | 22 | 1 |
| _Thermite | startTradingTimeShort | 5 | 50 | 1 |
| _Thermite | stopTradingTime | 30 | 90 | 1 |
| _Thermite | fastMa | 600 | 1000 | 20 |
| _Thermite | slowMa | 600 | 1300 | 30 |

In the initial back-test I ran on Tradestation, I stepped seven parameters for a total of 2950 tests on data going back to 1997, the start of the E-mini S&P 500. My goal was to provide the WFO software that comes with Tradestation ample wiggle room as the S&P 500 drifts slightly over time. I had the computer look at different stop loss settings, times to enter and exit trades, as well as moving average filters.

But still, the question remains: How much data should we test? Should we test three years? Ten years? How much out-of-sample data should we test? Should we test 20% as I suggested, or should we test 30%? In effect, we are building a matrix of possibilities. Here is a screenshot from the Walk-forward Optimizer that comes with Tradestation:

Cluster Analysis: Matrix of Multiple Walk-Forward Analyses

|  | Start | Stop | Increment |
|---|---|---|---|
| Out-Of-Sample % | 10 | 30 | 5 |
| Walk Forward Runs | 4 | 20 | 4 |

☑ Prescribe # of Walk-forward runs     ☐ Anchored

I wanted to test out-of-sample data from 10% to 30%, with each move incremented by five percent. Next, I set the number of walk-forward runs from four to twenty. At this point, I want to visually show you how to picture each walk-forward run.

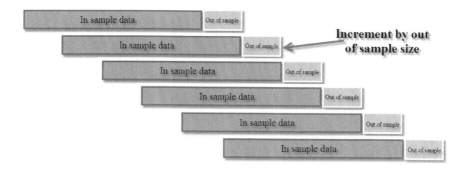

Starting at the beginning of the E-mini data in 1997, each test will look at a portion of the data, test the trading rules in-sample, then test a portion of the data out-of-sample. The start of the next test's in-sample data will be incremented by the out-of-sample data size and so on for as many tests as are selected. I selected five tests for this example, which in effect creates twenty-five tests to run on the WFO.

| OOS% \ Runs | 4 | 8 | 12 | 16 | 20 |
|---|---|---|---|---|---|
| 10 | PASS | PASS | PASS | PASS | PASS |
| 15 | PASS ** | PASS | PASS | PASS | PASS |
| 20 | PASS | PASS | PASS | FAILED | FAILED |
| 25 | PASS | PASS | PASS | FAILED | FAILED |
| 30 | PASS | FAILED | FAILED | FAILED | FAILED |

Each test will find the best parameter from the 2950 possible combinations of inputs. So now we're up to 73,750 total back-tests. Talk about computer intensive! Notice that a "pass" or "fail" grade is given to each walk-forward test. The test criterion is based on several options. The option that I want you to pay attention to is criterion number two, walk-forward efficiency. Efficiency greater than 50% between in-sample and out-of-sample data is preferred. In Chapter 5, a portion of the Trading System Score equation was dedicated to a similar ratio. You want to penalize a walk-forward test when out-of-sample testing isn't coming close to in-sample.

Trading a system that can't survive the scrutiny of this magnitude of testing means it will surely die in a great ball of flame when it is traded in the ever-changing markets of the future.

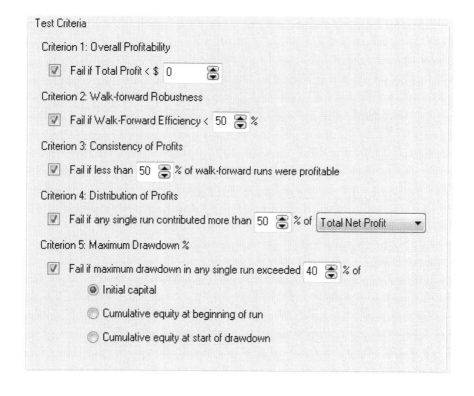

If you look once again at the cluster analysis I showed on the previous page, you will see that as more tests are run, the higher the likelihood of the walk-forward test failing. The answer as to why this occurs is simple. As you increase the number of walk-forward runs, you decrease the amount of data available for back-testing. As it turns out, the WFO found the best efficiency clustered around eight runs and 15% out-of-sample data. That results in just over six years of data needed for optimization. The suggested re-optimization time is every 392 days, about once a year. I ran this walk-forward cluster analysis back in 2012. As I write this, I'm just about due for my next optimization. What I will do is go back into Tradestation and step the same parameters I showed you before. However, I will not be using any out-of-sample data this time. I will simply use 2233 days of E-mini data when I optimize to find the best parameters.

Re-optimization schedule: (In-Sample=3728 days, Out-Of-Sample=410 days)

|  | Current | OOS+1 | OOS+2 | OOS+3 |
|---|---|---|---|---|
| Date | 2012/06/06 | 2013/07/21 | 2014/09/04 | 2015/10/19 |

Don't be afraid of experimenting with different out-of-sample percentages and a higher number of tests. Here's an example from a cluster analysis I ran on a NASDAQ 100 trading system with thirteen years of data. Notice the clustering of passing grades near 10% out-of-sample and fifty walk-forward tests.

| OOS% \ Runs | 10 | 20 | 30 | 40 | 50 | 60 | 70 | 80 | 90 | 100 |
|---|---|---|---|---|---|---|---|---|---|---|
| 1 | PASS | PASS | PASS | PASS | PASS | PASS | PASS | PASS | PASS | FAILED |
| 2 | PASS | PASS | PASS | PASS | FAILED | FAILED | FAILED | FAILED | FAILED | FAILED |
| 3 | PASS | PASS | PASS | FAILED | FAILED | FAILED | PASS | PASS | PASS | PASS |
| 4 | PASS | PASS | FAILED | FAILED | PASS | PASS | PASS | PASS | PASS | PASS |
| 5 | PASS | FAILED | FAILED | PASS | PASS | PASS | PASS | PASS | PASS | PASS |
| 6 | PASS | FAILED | PASS | PASS | PASS | PASS | PASS | PASS | PASS | PASS |
| 7 | PASS | FAILED | PASS | PASS | PASS | PASS | PASS | PASS | PASS | PASS |
| 8 | PASS | FAILED | PASS | PASS | PASS | PASS | PASS | PASS | PASS | PASS |
| 9 | FAILED | FAILED | PASS | PASS | PASS | PASS | PASS | PASS | PASS | PASS |
| 10 | FAILED | PASS | PASS | PASS | PASS | PASS | PASS | PASS | FAILED | PASS |
| 11 | PASS | PASS | PASS | PASS | PASS | PASS | PASS | PASS | PASS | PASS |
| 12 | FAILED | PASS | PASS | PASS | PASS | PASS | PASS | FAILED | PASS | PASS |
| 13 | FAILED | PASS | PASS | PASS | PASS | PASS | PASS | PASS | PASS | FAILED |
| 14 | FAILED | PASS | PASS | PASS | PASS | PASS | PASS | PASS | PASS | PASS |
| 15 | FAILED | PASS | PASS | PASS | PASS | PASS | PASS | PASS | | |

Right away, I want to let you know that developing a system on all historical data and then stress testing it with WFO is still data-snooping. We knew ahead of time that the WFO would find a solution because you likely would not try to test a system that didn't already pass casual back-testing of 80% in-sample, 20% out-of-sample. The way I see it though is that the system was robust in the first place. I would rather trade a system that has proven its edge time and time again since it began trading. If that's not possible, then my simple rule of thumb is to test on at least ten years of data for intraday systems. The Thermite trading system we've been using as an example has been robust on 16 years of data. I've been trading it profitably since 2008. That's nearly five years of the toughest environment any system must face – the future. You need systems that will stand the test of time, that function amidst chaos, not a flash in the pan.

One thing you might want to experiment with is increasing the number of runs while decreasing the out-of-sample percent. This will give you many more tests for robustness of your re-optimization interval. Ideally, the more often you re-optimize, the quicker you will adapt to the markets. In nature, it's not actually survival of the fittest, it survival of the quickest to adapt. Trading is the same way. If I had access to the Tradestation WFO source code, I would absolutely love to test what happens when you re-optimize ten years of data once a month. Heck, why not every day? As a matter of fact, I know of a trader that re-optimizes after every trade he makes. That trader is me. I must admit I only do this for one system that uses tick charts and an avalanche of data.

Let's now move to advanced techniques for using WFO and the switches I talked about earlier. I like radical ideas, so perhaps this failed experiment will serve as a catalyst for an idea of yours that does work.

One of the more popular ideas of Richard Dennis, Bill Eckhardt, and their Turtle Traders was to buy n-period breakouts. They would simply buy at 20-day highs and sell at 20-day lows. Basically, they wanted to buy as long as the futures contract was going up, and give the trade some leeway to account for random fluctuations in price.

I decided to design a system that would buy on n-day breakouts, and then sell on n-day breakdowns. I stepped each parameter from two to thirty. I did the same for shorting. The extra twist you might find interesting is I added switches that would turn off buying or turn off selling short. I knew that gold has had many bull and bear markets. Instead of filtering out long/short trades with a moving average, I decided to use a brute force method. The WFO test would find the best set of parameters to use. One of those parameters could be a switch that turns off short selling or going long. Amazingly, a large test of 80 runs was profitable and passed the robustness test, but I didn't like the results enough to trade it with my money.

I have one last tip for you before I leave the subject of walk-forward testing. There are only a few fitness functions you can select to judge which parameters are the "best" during an in-sample run. If I had my way, I would use the significance function I showed you earlier which combines profit factor, the square root of the number of trades, and the ratio of net profit to worst drawdown. Since that is not an option, let's create a weighted fitness between net profit and the Tradestation index (Net profit * winners / max drawdown).

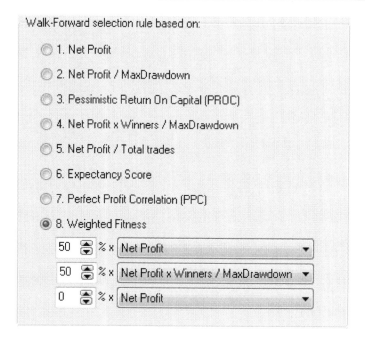

I'll admit there are many more rabbit holes you can go down from here, such as genetic programming. But I wrote this book more as a guide, to show you where you should go for immediate progress. I don't want to waste your time – or mine – with an enormous encyclopedia of possible stories to follow. I want to keep this baby lean and mean. The guiding principle of this book is for you to succeed as quickly as possible, to live the life of the 10x trader, and for a few other reasons I've hinted at already, and which are outlined at the end of this book. So let's move on.

# Chapter 6

*Men who reject the responsibility of thought and reason*

*can only exist as parasites on the thinking of others.*

*- Ayn Rand*

### Taking Action: Ready, Fire, Aim!

The journey of 1000 miles starts with that first step. So now it's up to you to take action. I've done my part, I've laid out a tried and tested plan for you to take that first step. Believe me, once you build momentum, once the results start pouring in, it's hard to stop. That momentum can start with one little step. Don't worry about doing everything perfectly. The most important thing is to take action. "Ready, fire, aim," as the saying goes.

There is no substitute for hands-on learning, so go open an account, and start using the software. Just take it the only way you can, one step at a time. Trust me, if you can follow a recipe in a cookbook, you can learn how to trade. Just make sure you follow the recipe to the letter, and make sure to check your emotional baggage at the door.

If you choose not to use what I've outlined for you here, then I can promise you more of the same. You'll be frustrated and flustered when your best-laid trading plan turns into yet another losing trade. Your dreams of an early retirement will be seriously in question. Your free time will continue to shrivel and deflate. Working into your advanced years will be the only option. Leading a 10x Trader Lifestyle™ will not be possible for you.

If, on the other hand, you choose to follow the 10x Trader Lifestyle™, wealth will automatically be attracted to you. Why? Because you've decided to invest in you. You've dedicated yourself and taken personal responsibility for creating the best model of the world possible. The more you realize things for how they truly are – the more you accept certain limitations and shortcomings, realize that there is no Holy Grail, while embracing the tested ways and means to be the best trader possible – the more success and fulfillment you will find throughout your remaining years.

### The Most Dreaded Question...

The question I am most often asked is, naturally, the one I dread to answer. But I'll do my best.

"What's the minimum I can start with"?

Like I said, I hate that question, because giving you an answer would sound like an endorsement of going with a minimum. Those that do the minimum get minimum results.

Let me shed some light on the subject. A good friend of mine asked me that same question, so I turned it around and asked him, "How much you got?"

His answer, $11,000 – and that if he lost it, he wouldn't be too upset.

Do you see the glaring flaw in this kind of thinking? It wouldn't upset him to piss away $11,000. What amount would make him flaming mad if he lost it all? If you don't care about the money you invest, you won't care when you screw up and lose it all. That's how accounts get blown out and people go bust. Wall Street pros and Casino operators amass fortunes on this quirk of humanity.

My reluctant answer to the "minimum amount" question is whatever amount would piss you off – and I mean really piss you off, in hair pulling, swearing at the computer fashion - if you lost it all. My buddy's final answer was $40,000. That was his number, so that should be his minimum.

So what's yours? No financial planner, and certainly not me, can answer that question for you.

When you care about the hard-earned money you're putting at risk, the hard sting of a trading mistake has an immediate result – it keeps you from turning that bad trade into an even worse trade.

Here's an example. Another friend of mine was trading the E-mini S&P 500. There was some sort of screw up and he was in a position when he should have exited. I asked why he didn't sell right that instant, since there was clearly no edge in keeping the trade open.

All he could do was shrug. He had no rational answer as to why he was in the trade. His decision was purely emotional. He didn't want to take a loss. His ego was not seeing that the end goal is, and must always be, to survive to trade another day. Finally, my friend did the right thing and got out. The market took a nosedive the very next day. As you can well imagine, he never made that mistake again. We humans are fast learners when it comes to pain. Touch a hot stove once is all it takes.

# Chapter 7

*Opportunity is missed by most people because it is dressed*

*in overalls and looks like work.*

*- Thomas A. Edison*

## A Missing Piece of the Puzzle

Okay, so here we are, guys, and still no promise of a Golden Fleece or Holy Grail. But you were supposed to forget about those already. Let those pipe dreams go up in smoke and blow away in the wind. Instead, let's focus on a recent change in technology that could easily save you $12,500 per year or more, opening a virtual Pharaoh's Tomb of trapped wealth for those of you with the technology to stake your claim. Listen carefully. Fund managers are leaving millions of bucks on the table due to their wasteful trading habits, and I can show you how to transfer some of that money from their accounts into yours, using this recent breakthrough in automated trading.

But be warned: Those of you who do not heed this message are doomed – yes, doomed – to failure, just like the multi-million dollar industry that is about to get wiped off the map due to this technology. So take everything we've learned so far, combine it with what follows, and get that much closer to living the auto-trader lifestyle, for you and your family.

## Tracking the Elephants – And Don't Forget Your Shovel

Ever since Robert Royce, "the Mayor of Silicon Valley," and Nobel Laureate Jack Kilby invented the microchip back in

1958, the exponential growth of technology has led not only to many new, exciting and extraordinary industries, but, at the same time, has completely over-hauled and revamped traditional ones too.

In this dizzying wake of change, entire industries have been practically washed away, leveled to the ground, gutted, and rendered obsolete, all by changes in technology (think of Polaroid, once a great American institution). Then again, others have gone from an obscure start-up to $1 billion in two years (see, for instance, the Instagram phenomenon).

It should come as no surprise that **trading technology is no exception** to the new economy's inevitable exponential growth, along with what I like to call "creative destruction." Indeed, trading technology is a direct beneficiary of this tidal wave of change. You see, there's been **a major change in technology that no one is talking about**, one that directly benefits you, while simultaneously exposing a fatal flaw in a multi-million dollar industry.

Earlier, I outlined the *do's* and *don'ts* of automated trading from the inside, from the perspective of someone who's experienced its ups and downs – namely, yours truly. The buck stops here. I showed you many of the mistakes that the amateur automated traders make, whether under-estimating slippage, or over-estimating the reliability of Internet providers, or the many flaws in popular trading strategies. I delivered the sobering fact that there is no Holy Grail, no single trick or secret, to this business. Adapt or die is the motto to trade by. Now let's add another equally important idea to the list: why are there edges in the first place?

Start by closing your eyes for a second and imagining that you're one of the ten thousand or so people, across this globe of ours, one who controls the lion's share of the money out there. **You have millions of dollars – maybe billions – under management**. Feels good, right? Now imagine that money is yours, all yours, to do with it as you please. It's your call entirely. So where would you invest? Which markets could even support investments of the magnitude your fund controls?

These questions would be answered as quickly as you started making trades. Your massive fund would move stocks around just as easily as it would an empty plastic bag on a windy day. Once you learned that vital lesson – namely, how easy it is to move stocks around but how tricky it is to allocate them all at once, with potentially devastating results – you'd be careful with your trading, right?

For one thing, you'd find more liquid assets to trade. You'd be much more likely to use unconventional orders such as "icebergs," which are basically one large order divided up into several smaller ones – you see only the "tip" at play, and not the mass of solid ice moving underneath. This way you don't show your hand to the rest of those hovering, salivating, bloodthirsty Wall Street sharks.

Now imagine once again that you're a fund manager of other people's money (OPM). Would you care as much about making perfect trades? Well, study after study shows that traders making buy decisions with their own money are much more prudent than those making buy decisions with other people's money. Look no further than the sorry shape of government spending, of ballooning Washington waste, with our hard-earned tax dollars, to see this effect at work. How many trillion are we in debt? I gave up counting years ago.

A single fund has the potential to move a solitary stock for several days. A single fund, all by its lonesome self, can move entire asset classes for minutes or even hours on end. Some of you might not know this, but a single fund (LTCM, or Long Term Capital Management, out of Greenwich, CT) nearly crashed the entire derivatives market in the 1998 crash all by itself.

It's worth considering this for a moment. LTCM was put together in 1993, and the minds they brought in made up a veritable dream team, including Myron Scholes and Robert Merton, two PhDs who went on to win the Nobel Prize in Economics in 1997, a year before the chaos, precisely for "a new method to determine the value of derivatives." Yet they overestimated the liquidity of the markets they were trading. They went from initially raking in 40% annual returns – after fees! – to losing $4.6 billion in a few months, which brought in Greenspan and the intervening Federal Reserve.

What these Nobel laureates had in IQ, they lacked in market wisdom – and they over-leveraged themselves, taking $5 billion in equity and borrowing $125 billion from the banks. They were in 25:1 at the outset. And who predicted that Russia would default on their government bonds back in the summer of 1998? Not those MIT professors, that's for sure.

What's enlightening – and infuriating – is when funds such as LTCM tank like that, they are forced to unload all their good assets too, so the S&P, gold, real estate – everything takes a plunge. There goes the damn baby along with the bathwater. It's not a pleasant thing to watch, and sure as hell not experience.

Traders, especially new traders, do this all the time, employing insane leverage. And why do they, the LTCMs, fail? In a large part because they don't accept that something unforeseen will eventually happen. They're like that turkey, remember – the one who is content day in and day out because he's warm and dry and well fed, oblivious to the approach of Thanksgiving.

Want some more proof? Take a close look at this chart below: you'll see three unrelated markets that dropped during the Flash Crash of 2010: the S&P 500, corn, and crude oil. All three fell intraday, even though the three markets weren't related.

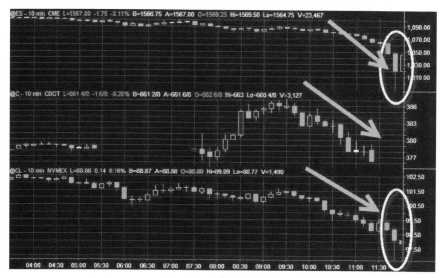

Selling, as you can see, attracted more sellers. That's actually a great strategy, one that takes advantage of people's natural desire to follow the herd. Eventually, participants are forced to liquidate. Margin calls, stop losses hit. It can get real ugly.

So now you know the stakes with these big boys, and how they can fall. But for now, let's drift back to our dream scenario. With your eyes closed, it's you in the driver's seat. Imagine <u>thousands</u> of these funds, controlling trillions of dollars of other people's money. With such figures involved, imagine the **enormous amount of <u>waste</u>** that follows, as fund managers make decisions to enter or exit stocks or asset classes like oil, silver, bonds, or other commodities, even soy beans. How many millions are we talking about here? Better still, how many billions? Use your imagination. The mind boggles.

Now picture these funds as huge, lumbering, lovable elephants. But instead of the usual stinking mess dropping from the rear of these massive beasts, instead imagine

enormous wads of $100 bills and Euros notes, of gold

Krugerrands and silver bars.

All we need to do, as savvy auto-traders, is carry

around a shovel and scoop up all these endless, odorless

riches...but not with just any shovel. Our "shovel" is a

computer, which we've programmed to look for the

numerous inefficiencies in the various markets. This computer

of ours automatically makes the trades, and then repeats the process repeatedly, scooping up all this gilded, glittering excess along the way. Sounds good, right?

While I was writing an earlier draft of this book, not too long ago, Tradestation had only just released a new version of their platform. Rather unceremoniously, they simply added a new feature and I didn't think much about it…that is, until it hit me like a ton of bricks, or better still, a vault full of gold bars. **"This changes everything,"** I thought, actually shaking my head in disbelief about what I'd nearly missed. Even the trading forums had little to nothing to say about this sudden change, let alone its implications for the Big Picture I suddenly envisioned before me.

### Ah-Ha!

Now before I unveil my grand "ah-ha" revelation, it's best to take a step back and tell you about the technology that was added to the most popular trading package around, one that wasn't available just a few months ago: Tradestation finally gives you the ability to drill down and look at prices all the way to the second. That's right: now you can use "second" charts in addition to minute charts, and the dozen other ways you can view and calculate prices. *On the surface, this doesn't seem at all newsworthy.* Hedge funds, after all, have had this technology for years. I mean, who cares if you can create fifty-nine second bar charts instead of a one-minute bar? What's the big deal?

And then my question hit me, as if a light bulb went on above my head and the clouds parted above. The one thing I had worried about most when it comes to automated trading execution – the thing that kept me up nights, scratching my head, has now, quickly and quietly, been downgraded from a Category 5 hurricane to a mild tropical storm. Finally, retail traders have another arrow in their quiver to reduce slippage, that all-important difference between a trade's expected price and what it actually trades for, which is more often than not worse than your system estimates…

...And the potential is much greater than I ever realized. It's going to allow all of us automated traders to make millions more than I ever thought possible. What this has done, at the same time, is reinforce my conviction, which I can't emphasize enough, that **the only thing that can be guaranteed is that things are going to change.** Things you once held dear and thought permanent, will fall victim to entropy. They will shrink, shrivel up, and be rendered obsolete. **That, I can promise you.** So, hold on and remember this...

Slippage is the death of any and all day trading models. When you're trading in and out of a position, over the course of a few minutes or hours, a string of bad fills can turn what you thought was a winning system into a losing one. You must be vigilant, constantly recording your real-world fills to see how they compare to your estimates. This is especially true for those trading large accounts or thinly traded markets or widely followed systems. And when thinking about systems, never forget that...

**The Problem isn't the System....It's the Execution of the System**

After nearly two decades in the trenches, I understand these flaws only too well. I'm not just a system designer, but I've purchased other commercially available systems. Most are over-optimized to prior data, but there are a few, admittedly, with merit. One of these systems I bought traded E-mini Russell 2000 futures. The Russell doesn't have near the liquidity of the S&P 500 (which often has 1000 or more contracts at the bid and ask), but it's still respectable, at perhaps 7% the liquidity of what the S&P 500 has to offer.

The system I was using traded early in the morning, when liquidity's supposed to be better than average. Unfortunately, when my strategy placed the buy order, I'd see prices rocket upwards, as if someone was looking over my shoulder and knew what I was doing. Reviewing the order book, **I saw a mad blur of new trades entering the market, all**

**within what must have been an actual millisecond.** I'd get these extremely bad fills – 5, 6, even 7 ticks higher than I should have been getting. Adding insult to injury, the market would then settle down as I watched prices move back to where they were just before. **The problem, it dawned on me, wasn't the system. It was the execution of the system.** Those who had bought the system along with me were trading at the exact same instant. Not the exact same minute, not the exact same second – but the exact same instant! We're talking milliseconds here, people. The speed of light.

All of a sudden, trading with everyone else in these less liquid markets became totally impractical. I had no choice but to stop trading them, or else watch as yet another $3000 goes down the drain. Fortunately, I learned an invaluable lesson: **Concentrate primarily on highly liquid markets like the S&P 500.** To this day, the S&P 500 is where I focus most of my efforts. It offers more liquidity than any other market in the world, bar none, including any single Forex pair. But not so fast. Up ahead, I'll tell you why even this seemingly logical conclusion was a mistake.

But first, let's back up for a moment, for a little perspective. The problem with the strategies I'd bought was that too many orders were dumped into the market at once, in just a fraction of a second – which is something I like to call **mobage** (not to be confused with the gaming app with the same name). And no, don't go googling the word – you'll only find it here. And it's a real important one to remember.

## Mob + Slippage = Mobage

Occasionally, a mob can be a force of good. Throughout history they've been able to overthrow repressive governments and corrupt kings. But they can often be dangerous and unruly, and sometimes it's good to see them dispersed with hoses and teargas. But when they march in and make a mess of our business, I'd switch from rubber to real bullets if I could. But instead we've got to bite the bullet and find a way to adapt to the damn crowd. I'll never accept the maxim "Mob rules."

So, back to "mobage." When it comes to my stop loss being hit, I can live with some slippage – it's part of the game. But slippage on the entry too? Sorry, that's just not going to cut it. We're in this game for one reason, to make money. So what I need is to have my orders spread out from the rest of the surly mob. Even a second or two would make a huge difference, turning an unprofitable system back to a profitable one, as long as the 100 other people using the system would just trade at slightly different times – even in less liquid markets like the Russell 2000. And now for...

## The Cure

If a system normally uses one-minute bars, why not use 59-second bars? Or 57? Or even 63? If a system normally uses 15-minute bars, try using 893-second bars (that's 14 minutes, 53 seconds). It really doesn't matter, as long as you're within a few seconds of the bar size the system was tested on. Whether you're trading right before 15 minutes or right after won't impact results all that much.

The key, the cure, to avoiding mobage, is simple: trade when the others are not. Once a week you could even pick up a six-sided dice, roll it, and add or subtract to your chart based on whatever number popped up. If you're using a 15-minute chart, like the one in my example, and you roll a 3, you could setup your chart to use 897-second bars. And if you're feeling real cheeky, roll the dice again, and if an odd number comes up, subtract seconds from the chart. If the number comes up even, add seconds to the chart.

This little tip, folks, will likely save you a ton of frustration and many thousands of dollars, many of your hard-earned bucks that would otherwise be lost to the "mob." A six-figure account, for example, could easily save **$12,500 per year** with this strategy alone.

You should also combine this with the tip I shared with you earlier, demonstrating how to save a bunch of money by placing a limit order that will automatically turn into a market order after however many seconds you tell Tradestation. I made a king's ransom with my Serendipity trading system by using that order type. But instead of merely placing my limit order at the closing price of the tick bar, I'd place it <u>one tick below</u>. *More often than not, I'd get filled at that price.* That's what I like to call **positive slippage**. Trading with positive slippage, people, is trading smart!

Let's take another look at the dice example. That's not exactly automated, now is it? And while it works, it doesn't live up to the 10x Trader Lifestyle I've presented to you. You should cut down on these tedious, mind-numbing chores because, in the end, they're like holes in a bucket. The more holes in your bucket, the less water you'll be able to fish out of the well. In fact, if you're not careful, you might end up bone dry, parched and poor. In this case, the "well" is the market and the "water" the money – YOUR MONEY – the hard-earned returns meant to change your life around for the better.

If you're the industrious type, you could create a function in Tradestation that would setup a delay of "n" number of seconds before the trade is executed. Heck, why stop there. Instead of delaying two seconds, why not delay the trade 2.07 seconds? That's a bit of high frequency trading for you.

Let's take this even deeper down the rabbit hole leading to Wonderland. Let's not just setup a delay, let's make it a **random number,** so someone doesn't walk in on you while you're rolling the dice in front of your trading screen. Talk about getting caught with your proverbial pants down, or inspiring confidence.

Your spouse might get the wrong idea and you'd be compelled to explain what I've been teaching you for the next hour. "No honey, I'm not using dice to make a trade decision...I mean I sort of...oh never mind!"

 **Bonus download**

Complementary anti-mobage software.

Download the system code for both delaying and randomly delaying a trade.

Point your browser to:

**www.10xtrader.com/skepticmobage**

Please take note of this – and I mean it. You should actually take notes and mark up the margins of this book. This is a working document, a blueprint for learning. Never forget!

I've showed you how to circumvent the serious problem of crowding in automated system trading. And this is only the most recent way for you to reach – and to maintain – the 10x trader lifestyle. That's what this whole book has been about. You might even be able to use this knowledge to get in before other traders get their signals. Perhaps you can even resurrect a dead system or two. Trading at unconventional times will be key as your account grows larger and larger. I've showed you this before with tick charts, but some of my best systems use time-based charts, including the still uber-profitable Thermite model.

## The End, With a Challenge

That's right, we've come to the end – but to the beginning, perhaps, of a new career for some of you. Thanks for the time you've spent with me here… Give yourself a pat on the back, because you deserve it. Most people spend more time deciding which computer to buy than they invest in increasing their trading knowledge.

For those of you with photographic memories – I'm jealous. And you, and only you, most likely remember that in the opening pages of this book I discussed some Italian toads that were able to predict an earthquake, and in the process saved their hides from certain death. Well, I'd like to end with another analogy from the natural world, along with a challenge.

First, let's talk about bees. Truly extraordinary creatures. Did you know that a typical bee colony can search six or more kilometers from their hive, and if a flower patch is within two kilometers of the hive, they have better than a 50% chance of finding it.

How? They send out scout bees, and when they find a strong source of nectar they head back to the hive and do a waggle dance, its intensity shaped somehow by the quality of the nectar they've returned with. The dance will attract others foragers, and the word, so to speak, spreads in an almost perfect fashion.

So basically the hive doesn't find the best nectar sources by sitting around and debating and considering all the possible alternatives and then determining an ideal foraging pattern. Instead, it sends out these scouts in dozens of different directions, trusting that at least one will find a first-rate patch, make it back safely, and dance with the talent of a Mick Jagger or Fred Astaire, so the hive will know where the food source is.

It's a two-fold process: first, uncover the possible alternatives (or flower patches) and then decide among them (who's the best dancer). And by sending out as many scout bees as possible, the hive will increase the odds of finding the best nectar source.

Are you catching on here, careful readers? Herein lays my challenge to you, and others. Spread the word, please. Since there are so many solutions to trading systems out there, no one can do it all; believe me, I've tried. So here's the challenge, the contest....Show me, show us, what you've got. What you've learned, of course – your knowledge – but also your instincts, your tenacity, your skepticism, your willingness to fail and pick yourself back up and keep plugging away.

As I hinted at in the beginning of this book, I'm calling it the Quant Prize, and it's worth $25,000, and if all goes well – and right now it's looking that way – this will be the first of many such contests.

This is about more than just money or bragging rights – although let's admit it, both are good motivators. When it comes to selecting the "best" system, we'll rely on the opinion of the crowd, which tends to get it right in these sort of situations. We'll have certain minimums, so the crowd will vote on only the top systems – a bit of weeding out is inevitable.

And if you want to compete it doesn't matter if you, the trader, are young or old, a valedictorian fresh out of college or a high school dropout, an idiot savant or a celebrated Wall Street guru. All that matters is performance, pure and simple. You know, one of my best systems was an accidental discovery, when I transposed two numbers that I created when just starting out. So you never know.

The prizewinner can use the cash for seed money to compound their account even faster. And the competition will force the system designer to become laser-focused because it has a deadline. But even if you don't want to compete, follow along and be sure to vote. I imagine somewhere down the road, I'll end up revising this book – the nature of this business almost ensures that. Or maybe write another one. But until then, they'll be plenty of webinars and articles and news flashes on my website, and not just the contest.

I imagine, with everything you've learned here, you can hit the ground running and design something exciting, profitable, and even revolutionary. I'm here to help you, to get those creative juices flowing, that ambition burning, and make your mark, your name, your fortune. Show me what you've got.

**Quick tip**

Visit the website now to learn more and enter the Quant Prize.

Point your browser to:

**www.10xtrader.com/skepticbook**

You're here for a reason – you want to win, in a profession where most lose.

That's a vast pool to profit from, but it's also a warning. Take the knowledge you have learned within these pages and create your own 10x Trader Lifestyle™.

Trade smart,

Dan Murphy

Made in the USA
Lexington, KY
28 June 2013